Fingerpicking Fiddle Tunes

Arranged for Fingerstyle Guitar

A systematic approach to the playing of Fiddle Tunes on guitar.
Learn Hoedowns, Reels, Set Tunes, Marches, Hornpipes,
Jigs, Strathspeys and Airs from a pioneer of the style.

By Ken Perlman

Cover Photo – Susanne Even
Cover Design – Shawn Brown
Layout and Pasteup – Kenny Warfield
Production – Ron Middlebrook

ISBN 1-57424-128-1
SAN 683-8022

Author's Bio

Ken Perlman is a well-known guitar and banjo player on the American and international folk music scene. His playing has taken him across North America, to the U.K., Western Europe and even Australia. He is considered a pioneer in adapting traditional Celtic and Southern dance music (usually referred to as *fiddle tunes*) to fingerstyle guitar. His solo recordings include *Northern Banjo* (Copper Creek), *Island Boy* (Wizmak), *Devil in the Kitchen* (Marimac), *Live in the U.K.* (Halshaw), and *Clawhammer Banjo and Fingerstyle Guitar Solos* (Folkways).

Ken's other guitar books include *Fingerstyle Guitar* and *Advanced Fingerstyle Guitar* (both from Centerstream Music). He has recorded the *Fingerstyle Guitar* companion video for Centerstream; he is guitar columnist for *Sing Out!* magazine, and he has written on guitar instruction for a number of other periodicals, including *Acoustic Guitar* and *Acoustic Musician.*

Ken's banjo books include *Clawhammer Style Banjo* (Centerstream), *Melodic Clawhammer Banjo* (Music Sales), *Everything You Wanted to Know about Clawhammer Banjo* (Mel Bay) and *Basic Clawhammer Banjo* (Mel Bay). He has recorded the *Clawhammer Style Banjo* video companion for Centerstream, as well as other audio and video banjo- instruction series for Mel Bay and Homespun.

Ken has produced several works devoted to "old-time" (traditional) fiddling on Prince Edward Island in the Canadian Maritimes. These include a tune book called *The Fiddle Music of Prince Edward Island: Celtic and Acadian Tunes in Living Tradition* (Mel Bay), an anthology cassette called *The Old Time Fiddlers of Prince Edward Island* (Marimac), and a two-CD anthology entitled *The Prince Edward Island Style of Fiddling* (Rounder Records).

He lives and works in the Boston area.

Preface to the Centerstream Edition

Fingerpicking Fiddle Tunes was first published over two decades ago. Now that Centerstream is making it available again, this is a good opportunity to look at the book anew, and to reflect upon its role in contemporary instrumental folk music instruction.

When the book first came out, playing traditional Celtic and Southern dance music (often called *fiddle tunes*) on fingerstyle guitar was quite rare. I had to work out the style and techniques presented in these pages on my own.

Fingerpicking Fiddle Tunes was the first modern book to present a systematic approach to the playing of fiddle tunes on fingerstyle guitar. Of course, it was customary as far back as the Renaissance for fretted-instrument players to compose settings for folk dance tunes, and the approach they used was not dissimilar to the one used here. This practice had been out of fashion for centuries, however, and I was in fact unaware of this historical precedent until long after I had come up with my own approach.

This was also the first modern folk music book to use a coherent and workable system of guitar tablature that included rhythm notation. Prior to the publication of *Fingerpicking Fiddle Tunes*, the writing of folk-guitar "tab" was fairly haphazard. In those bad old days, most guitar tab lacked rhythm notation (indications for half, quarter or eighth notes etc). Most tab-writers were also unclear about the location of upbeats and downbeats, inconsistent about the number of beats per measure, and inaccurate in terms of such rhythmic subtleties as ornamentation and syncopation. What's more, there was a general tendency towards carelessness: if a guitarist wasn't already familiar with a tune, he or she usually had little chance of learning it properly from the notation alone.

By including rhythm notation, being careful about measures, upbeats, and downbeats, and by making a special effort to represent arrangements precisely, this book succeeded – probably for the first time – in accurately representing folk-guitar settings. It also set a standard that other compilers of instruction books were quick to emulate.

The new publisher and I decided to expand this new edition by roughly 25% and include eleven new arrangements – all of which are selections I have recorded over the years on the following LPs and CDs: *Clawhammer Banjo and Fingerstyle Guitar Solos* (Folk ways), *Devil in the Kitchen* (Marimac), *Island Boy* (Wizmak) and *Northern Banjo* (Copper Creek). Note that for these new tunes, there have been a few modifications in the tab and standard notational system employed: these are explained in an introduction to this new section.

Of late, there has been an upsurge of interest in playing fingerstyle fiddle tunes on guitar. Many recent arrangements have employed open tunings – most notably "Dad-gad" tuning (DADGAD). My own settings are in standard or "drop-D" (DADGBE) tunings, but I'm sure that once you've tried a few pieces, you'll agree that these tunings are equal, or even superior to open tunings as vehicles for the genre.

The arrangements in this book offer you an excellent opportunity to transfer the spirit and vitality of traditional Irish, Scottish, and Southern dance music to your instrument. I hope you enjoy playing them as much as I enjoyed creating my approach to the style!

Ken Perlman
Arlington, Massachusetts

Table of Contents

CD Track List

The accompanying CD digitally reproduces one of the flexible plastic LPs that originally accompanied this volume (the original master recording was misplaced years ago by a previous publisher). Although I could have recorded a new version of this material, I felt that the spirit and enthusiasm exhibited in the playing – done when these arrangements were all freshly composed– far outweighted the obvious shortcomings in audio fidelity.

This CD illustrates only the thirty-one tunes that made up the original edition. Each of the eleven new arrangements in this edition appears on one of my recordings – *Northern Banjo, Island Boy, Devil in the Kitchen* or *Banjo & Guitar Solos* - all of which can be obtained through my website, www.kenperlman.com

Introduction

I had been playing the guitar for some time before the idea of playing fiddle tunes in finger style even occurred to me. Sure I'd heard Doc Watson's flashy flatpicking arrangements of bluegrass favorites, but though I enjoyed listening to them, it was somehow never my style. I've always been a finger-picker, and from the time I first heard Dylan's haunting arrangement of "Boots of Spanish Leather," and Dave Van Ronk's incredibly imaginative treatment of both country and city blues, I had refused to play the guitar in any other way.

I started as a pattern picker. Pattern picking, also known as "Travis picking" (after Merle Travis), or "Cotton picking" (after Elizabeth Cotton), is a style where the fingers play the treble strings in different combinations over an alternating bass laid down by the thumb.[1] Although the idea behind it is simple, pattern picking can become a highly expressive and interesting way of playing the guitar. Dylan, Pat Sky and Tom Paxton were all pattern pickers in their heyday. In a highly elaborate form, John Fahey and Leo Kottke are pattern pickers.

The problem with pattern picking is that you must unlearn habits that have become second nature in order to play other types of music. When I discovered traditional blues around the end of 1969, the playing of Robert Johnson, Willie McTell, Skip James and others quickly captured my imagination, but my attempts to imitate their styles were handicapped by my pattern-oriented approach to music. While country-blues style varies tremendously from artist to artist, it basically involves a flexible treble line of sometimes great rhythmic complexity played against a steady bass with a strong "offbeat" (one TWO three FOUR) provided by the thumb. This bass could be alternating or played on one string as a drone. It took many months of listening to Mississippi John Hurt's records to master the "swing" characteristic of the alternating bass of country blues, to begin to free my fingers enough from what my thumb was doing to handle the new rhythms, etc. And yet, with all its increased flexibility, I found that I had to unlearn many aspects of blues picking in order to arrange two-part fiddle tunes.

My involvement with traditional fiddle music (or "old-timey" music, as it is often called) dates back to the night I took the battered banjo I had been fooling around with for three years down to the weekly local old-time musician's gathering (at the Unmuzzled Ox Coffee House in Ithaca, N. Y.) and found I could keep up on the five tunes I knew. I became a "clawhammering fool" overnight, and learned about fifty tunes of the Southern and New England repertoire in a few months. Since I couldn't get them out of my head, it wasn't very long before I tried out a few of the tunes on guitar, in finger style.

This proved more complicated than just transcribing the tunes from fiddle to guitar and adding an alternating bass. For as they are not so much "fiddle tunes" as music intended for folk

Dancers & Fiddler, c. 1925; courtesy New York Country Dance & Song Society.

---

1) Neither Travis nor Cotton was actually a pattern-picker, by the way. Both did however use a strong alternating bass, which the original pattern pickers may have studied when they developed the style.

dancing, these melodies had to be set on guitar in such a way that they could be danced to. This meant that a certain "lightness" of melody and steadiness of beat had to be attained, and that it had to be possible, within the guitar "setting," to play the tune at or at least near its proper tempo. I would like to outline the steps I followed in getting together a successful method of attack. It will help you understand how to approach these tunes:

- I tried playing all the melody notes with the fingers of the right (plucking) hand over an alternating bass, as John Hurt would have played them. (See "Old Joe Clarke," p. 13). Most fiddle tunes have too many notes for this approach, and the arrangements were slow, choppy and uninteresting.

- I got as many of the melody notes as possible by "plucking with the fretting hand" (hammering on, pulling off and sliding), holding on to the alternating bass. The speed and smoothness of the tunes improved here, but the right "sound" still eluded me. It took a few months to put my fretting hand in shape to do all this work.

- I began to unlearn standard chord positions. I soon realized that a two-part fiddle tune only requires two parts. It wasn't necessary to hold down a full chord at all times. Sometimes only two notes needed to be fretted. Sometimes new chord positions (involving some of the melody notes) needed to be invented. This "lightened" the sound of the arrangements considerably.

- I found I had to unlearn the alternating bass. This was very difficult indeed. After all, some fiddle tunes sounded very nice with a steady "ump-chuck" accompaniment. Many did not. I discovered that bass notes were often required only on the accented beats, and that sometimes a passage sounded best with no bass notes at all. My arrangements were now much less dense and began to sound like fiddle tunes.

Even with all these changes, something was still lacking from my arrangements. In order to make the tunes come alive on guitar, I had to first understand three things about the nature of fiddle music:

- *Differentiation by type of tune*—I had always thought of jigs separately, but had lumped reels, hoedowns, hornpipes and marches together in my head as "tunes in four." Recognizing that each had distinct requirements helped a lot in my arranging attempts.

- *Special accents*—Although all hornpipes, for example, are accented on the first and third beats, there will often be points in a *particular* hornpipe that will be specially accented and give the tune its character. This is, of course, also true of jigs, marches, reels etc., and must be taken into account when arranging a piece for guitar.

- *Phrasing*—This was the final step. I realized that a fiddle tune was not just a series of notes divided by measure lines, but a piece of music divided into note groupings or "phrases." It then became clear that the time to switch positions (see p. 8) was at the end of these phrases, and that each note had to be obtained in such a way as to maintain the phrase's integrity.

The versions of the tunes given here are pretty much as played by old-timey or Irish musicians of the American Northeast, and are almost always in the key that the fiddler would play them. I have tried not to "fudge" (simplify or change the melody to make the setting easier) so if the notes are slightly different from the version you know, it's mostly due to the folk process. (If there were parts of the melody I was unsure of, I tried to check them out with other musicians before finalizing the arrangements.)

Once you get the hang of it you should be able to keep up with a string band or "ceili" band[1] on most of these pieces, if they're played at "dancing speed." (Although there's no way you could keep up with, say, a Southern string band going full tilt. You'd have to flatpick for that.) I find it a lot of fun to play with one or two other instruments—say a wood flute, or a concertina and mandolin, or a tin whistle, or even a fiddle itself. Best of all, though, is the feeling that the guitar is really a band unto itself, and that you can capture all the beauty and liveliness of these tunes with your own two hands.

I play a small steel-string guitar with a 14-fret short-scale neck (better known as a Martin 00-18). I recommend guitars of this type or smaller for playing two-part fiddle tunes (12-fret necks are fine, maybe even better),[2] because the string tension is less and the treble more dominant. I also suggest that you hold the thumb of your fretting hand *behind* the neck when you're not using it to fret the sixth string, because it makes big stretches, hammering on and pulling off much easier.

I've set aside a few tunes for the purpose of teaching techniques (paralleling the way I learned the style), but the rest of them are arranged by type of tune. Before each section there will be some notes on how to approach playing the tunes in it (be sure to read them!), and within each section the tunes are arranged more or less in order of difficulty. Start on the simpler hoedowns and set tunes. Then try a jig or two. The reels and hornpipes should come last.

I hope that you find this book useful and that it will encourage you to make your own arrangements.

Ken Perlman

---

1) The ceili (pronounced kayley) band is the traditional Irish dance band, (see p. II).

2) I have never played a nylon-string guitar, but Gordon Bok does some fine 2-part fiddle tunes on his (Folk Legacy No. FS1-40), so if you have one—use it!

DaCosta Woltz's Southern Broadcasters, c.late 1920s. L to R: D. Woltz,
P. Goodson, B. Jarrel, F. Jenkins. Collection of Ray Alden.

The Tablature

I have rarely been able to learn from published tablature. You often need a good imagination and more patience than I'm capable of to figure out just what the tab writer is getting at. For example, pickup notes are rarely set off clearly at the beginning, so the whole piece ends up written completely out of phase. As a result, you have no idea where the accents are and the tune doesn't sound like anything. Or the writer won't be able to make up his mind about the number of beats in each measure. Sometimes there will be four beats, sometimes five, sometimes seven or eight. (One well-known book of clawhammer banjo tab whose name I won't mention is notorious in this respect.) When it comes to tab for finger-style guitar, where two parts are involved, the opportunities for confusion multiply. It can be ambiguous which notes are played by the thumb and which by the fingers. Or it can be unclear just how long to play each note, or where the finger notes come in relation to the thumb notes, etc.

The tablature system used in this book will astound you by the ease with which it can be read. Pickup notes, if any, will be clearly set off at the beginning of each piece. Each measure will have exactly the same number of beats (usually four), and the strongest melodic accent will always be at the beginning of each measure. There will be absolutely no confusion as to the time value of each note, or where and how it is to be played.

The "tab" will be written on a "staff" of six lines, each one corresponding to a string on the guitar. The highest line signifies the first string, the lowest the sixth, etc. Numbers on the lines show the fret to be pressed down. If 3 is placed on line 1, press down the first string, third fret. If 5 appears on line 3, press down the third string, fifth fret.

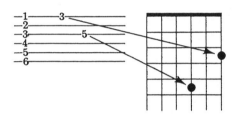

Time value for each note will be shown as follows:

0   half note = two beats

—   whole rest—don't play for four beats

▬   half rest—don't play for two beats

1   quarter note = one beat

♩   quarter rest—don't play for one beat

2   eighth note = ½ beat (two = one quarter note)

9

0   3   pair of eighth notes (up to four can be tied together in similar manner)

⌐   eighth rest—don't play for ½ beat (do not confuse with the number 7)

0•   3   dotted pair—played as two eighth notes, but the first getting much more emphasis (Dot-da)

0• or 1• or 2• (2•)   any note with a dot after it has its value increased by 50%. A dotted half = 3 beats. A dotted quarter = 1½ beats. A dotted eighth (see above) = ¾ beat.

0 2 4   triplet—three notes played in the space of one quarter note
   3

4   4   sixteenth note = ¼ beat (two = one eighth note). It's the other half of that dotted pair.
or

2   5   pair of sixteenth notes (up to four can be tied together in similar manner)

⌐   sixteenth rest—will only appear when a dotted pair is split up between thumb and fingers.

6   grace note—has no time value of its own but absorbs some of the note it is attached to. A very quick note.

0 2   double grace note—two very quick notes

When a note is to be plucked by the thumb, the line indicating time value will originate from the *bottom* of the staff. When a note is to be plucked by the fingers, the time value line will come from the *top* of the staff:

fingers

thumb

In either case, both the thumb-half of the staff *and* the finger-half of the staff will have *exactly* the same number of beats. When either the thumb or the fingers are to be idle, you'll see a rest. When more than one note is to be played simultaneously by *either* the fingers or the thumb, they will be contained in brackets (for less than 2 beats), or surrounded by a box (for two beats or more):

0 or 1
1   2

When a note is to be plucked by the fretting hand, it will be connected by a tie (⌣ or ⌢) to the note before and one of the following symbols will appear at the end of its time value line:

H

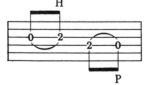

H = hammer on
P = pull off
SL = slide

P

If more than one note in a row is to be obtained in this manner the tie will reach from the plucked note to the last note connected to it:

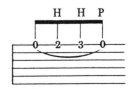

Fingering

Fingering will be indicated by a Roman numeral above the staff that shows *position.* A "II" above the staff means that the fretting hand should be moved to a position where the first finger plays the second fret. Then the second finger plays the third fret, the third finger plays the fourth fret and the fourth finger plays the fifth fret. This is called playing in second position. A "V" above the staff means that the whole hand must be moved up the neck to fifth position, where the first finger plays the fifth fret, the second finger plays the sixth fret, the third finger plays the seventh fret, etc. A "III" means move down the neck to third position. Continue playing in one position until directed to change to another.

Other fingering symbols

- Barre III - This means that the first finger of the fretting hand is placed across the entire neck of the guitar—at the third fret in this case. The passage is then played out of this position. Barre VII means the first finger goes across the seventh fret, etc.
- C, G, Am, Em, A7, D, F, etc. The passage is to be played while the fretting hand is holding down standard first position chords:

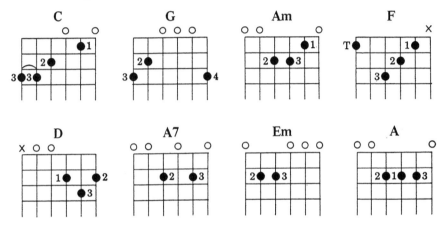

- Barre C-V or C7-III - Barre C-V means the standard chord is played under a barre at the fifth fret. C7-III means that the chord C7 is moved up to third position:

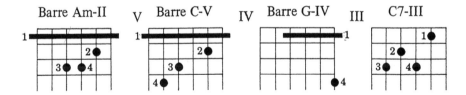

- If the thumb is to be used to fret the sixth string, a T will appear, in parentheses, next to the number.
- Positions not readily apparent from the tab will be diagrammed below each piece.

Time signatures

A time signature will appear next to the title of each piece. 6/8 time will appear in the jig section and 3/4 time will appear in the end section (both will be explained later), but most of the pieces will either bear the directions "common time" or "cut time." A common time piece (technically in 4/4) will cry out for four bass notes per measure because it has a strong feeling of four. I have written these out with a pair of eighth notes above each bass note. A cut time piece (technically in 2/2) has a very strong feeling of twoness and requires bass notes only on the first and third beats. (Think of a cut time measure as a swinging pendulum, with half the measure in each swing.) These have been written out as four linked eighth notes above each bass note.

Repeat signs

If a tune section is to be repeated, the symbol ‖: will appear at its beginning and the symbol :‖ will appear at its end. (Pickup notes occuring before a repeat sign are not played when the section is repeated.

First and second endings

The last measure of a tune section often differs slightly on each repetition. The first time through, the last measure leads you back to the beginning of the section. The second time through it leads you on to the beginning of the next section. In this case you will see the following notation:

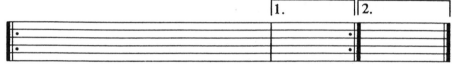

This means: Start at the beginning of the piece, and play until you see the symbol :‖, including the measure under bracket No. 1 (called the first ending). Then return to the symbol ‖:, play through the section again, *skip the measure under bracket No. 1,* and play the measure under bracket No. 2 (called the second ending). Then go on to the next section.

Phrasing

See pages 4 and 23 for a detailed discussion. When a new phrase starts at a point not co-inciding with the measure lines, I have divided off the staff as follows:

Special accents

When a note is to be given particular emphasis, I have placed the following symbol above it: ▼ (standard symbol = ➤)

Modes

Most of the music heard today (both classical and popular) is in the so-called "major" (Ionian) mode, which goes do-re-mi-fa-so-la-ti-do. This same "scale" can be played in seven different ways, or "modes," depending which syllable you start and end on. Since many folk songs and traditional dance tunes, including about one third of the tunes in this book, are in modes other than major, you should understand something about at least the three most common of them.

- The Aeolian (Ay-o-lee-an) mode, also known as "natural minor" starts and ends on "la," (la-ti-do-re-mi-fa-so-la). The mode we now call "minor" was invented in the seventeenth century, when the seventh note of the Aeolian scale ("so") was raised a semitone (one fret). Traditional tunes are almost never in the minor mode. If they sound "minor-ish," they are usually in Aeolian or Dorian, (see below). Minor melodies have accompaniments like Am-Dm-E, Dm-Gm-A, or Em-Am-B, while Aeolian melodies have accompaniments like Am-Dm-G, Dm-Gm-C, or Em-Am-D.

- The Dorian mode starts and ends on "re" (re-mi-fa-so-la-ti-do-re). Dorian is the mode most often played out of the banjo tuning known as "sawmill" or "mountain minor," and blues guitarists will recognize it as a blues scale with the third and seventh notes flat. Dorian tunes have accompaniments like Am-D-G, Dm-G-C, or Em-A-D.

- The Mixolydian mode starts and ends on "so," (so-la-ti-do-re-mi-fa-so). It's essentially a major scale with the seventh note flatted a semitone. Mixolydian tunes have accompaniments like G-F, A-G, D-C. Good Picking!

About the Music

Most of the music in this book developed as a distinct form around the middle of the eighteenth century, the way blues and jazz originated in the American South in the early part of the twentieth century. Its early growth coincided with the first great popularity of the fiddle and wood flute as dance-accompanying instruments. Before this period, dance music was either very much like, say, "The Return from Fingal" (p. 43) and played on the warpipes, or like the classical music of the Renaissance or Baroque periods, and played on the pipe and tabor.[1] Although we have no way of knowing how this new music was played in 1750, it is likely that, then as now, its distinguishing characteristic was a simple but driving rhythm, a trait that was much strengthened by the introduction of the piano to the dance band as a chording instrument around 1820. (It is curious that this simple driving rhythmic style came about at the beginning of the industrial revolution, whose technology had a rhythm of a similar sort.)[2]

By the end of the eighteenth century, fiddle music had crystalized into several forms, the most common of which were jigs, reels, hornpipes, set tunes and marches. Ordinarily, each of these tune-types consisted of two distinct but related parts ("A" and "B"), each eight measures in length. The A part stated the theme and was almost always lower in pitch than the B part, which answered the theme at a higher pitch, and ended in a bar or two reminiscent of the ending of part A. Both parts were usually played twice.

Jigs, reels and hornpipes (etc.) were never distinct dances in themselves, but were instead classes of tunes used to accompany two distinct dance styles: set dancing and step dancing. Set dancing involves several small groups ("sets") of dancers, within which all the figures of a dance are executed. (Square dancing is an American form of set dance.) Step dancing, sometimes called clogging, is done by an individual and usually involves figures of great complexity. (This is the ancestor of modern tap dancing.)

Jigs are written in 6/8 time, which means that each measure can contain as many as six eighth notes. These are played as two groups of three with the stronger accent on the first note of each of the two groups (DA-da-da, DA-da-da), so jigs always have a strong feeling of twoness about them (see p. 61).[3] They were originally meant to accompany step dances, but today, some Irish set dances and British "contradances"[4] are done to jigs as well. Northumbrian sword dancing has always been done exclusively to jig accompaniment.[5] If you haven't got the idea yet, two well known jigs are "The Irish Washerwoman," and "Garry Owen" (of "Little Big Man" fame). Hum them to yourself.

Reels and hornpipes are written in cut (2/2) time, and almost always have eight eighth notes per measure, arranged in two groups of four with the accent on the first note of each group,

---

1) The pipe, a thin, three holed recorder, was played with one hand by the musician, while he beat time with his other on the tabor, a small snare drum. These instruments are still used today to accompany Morris dancing in south-central England.

2) It is also interesting to note that this represented the last great European contribution (with the possible exception of the waltz) to dance music. Further developments were to derive from black culture in the American South.

3) There's a type of jig, called a slip jig, that's written in 9/8 time as three groups of three eighth notes, with the strongest accent on the first note of each group. Slip jigs have a strong feeling of threeness about them and are the probable ancestor of the waltz.

4) A type of English set dance.

5) Northumberland is a region in the northeast corner of England (near the Scots border). The dance involves a set of five men holding on to either end of five blunt-edged or two-handled swords as they execute complicated figures.

(DA-da-da-da, DA-da-da-da). There is some difficulty telling them apart, and American fiddlers treat them almost identically, but there are important differences in structure between the two. Basically, reels are used for set dancing. They must be played at considerable speed to come alive, and to give the proper "lift" necessary to the dances they are played for. Reels are often written so that the end of the B part leads back to the A to give the dancers a feeling of circularity. There is a liquidity, or sliding quality between notes, and pitch intervals between them tend to be small. Hornpipes were meant for step dancing and had to be played slow, so that complicated steps could be executed. They therefore had to sound "pretty" or at least interesting at the slower pace. Hornpipes tend to have larger pitch intervals between notes, and more complicated harmonies. They are often played with a "dotted feel" (with "dotted pairs" ♩. ♪, see p. 7), and each part will end with the heavy finality of three quarter notes (Dot-dot-Dot).

It took a long time to go through all the figures of a typical set dance, and it required a very skillful and tireless musician to keep a reel going at the proper pace for all that time. So, sometime in the late eighteenth century, musicians began using "set tunes" (called "polkas" in Ireland), which were built around a structure of four quarter notes per measure, with accents on the first and third (DOT-dot-DOT-dot), to accompany the set dances. Set tunes were often drawn, like "The Rose Tree" (p. 37) from the popular songs of the day.

Marches, although similar to set tunes in structure were not ordinarily used for dancing. They were tunes written for inspiring the soldiers of a particular clan or nation with proper military sentiments. Their melodies did, however, reflect the musical style of the dance tunes of the day, and sometimes a march would be played as a set tune, and vice versa.

Musicians in this country were playing most of the fiddle music of eighteenth-century Britain and Ireland as soon as it could be published and sent over on sailing ships. Until 1800, their musical styles and interests parallelled their European counterparts, and New England fiddling has changed little since then, except that hornpipes and reels are now played almost the same, and that jigs have pretty much fallen into disuse.

In the South, however, considerable change in dance, in instrumentation, and in the music itself occurred throughout the nineteenth century. To their own style of clogging and set (square) dancing, Southerners added circle dancing which involved maybe forty or more couples weaving about each other. The five-string banjo was introduced around 1850 and probably provided, as in modern times, a moving background of notes against which the fiddle played. Then, around 1910 the steel-string guitar came into vogue via the Sears-Roebuck catalogues of the day, and was used to provide a beat.[1] The biggest change, however, was in terms of musical accent. It seems that Southern musicians, being exposed to black or black-influenced music such as ragtime and cakewalks, began to accent the off-beat of their fiddle tunes. The new pattern then, for a reel or hornpipe (Southerners never had much use for jigs, either) was *da-da-DA-da, da-da-DA-da*. In the Southeast, fiddlers even developed a new type of bow stroke (the shuffle bow) that enabled them to bring the bow down hard on each offbeat to accent the rhythm. Old tunes were changed or new ones were composed to fit the new bowing pattern, and tunes that did not fit into shuffle bowing were discarded. This is the origin of the hoedown tunes.

The heavily ornamented virtuoso "Sligo style" most popular among Irish musicians today was brought to perfection in the 1920's by fiddlers like Sligo-born Michael Coleman, who lived most of his life, and did most of his recording in New York City. Until the advent of the Irish group "The Chieftains" in the late 1950's the traditional Irish dance band consisted of fiddle, wood flute and chording piano. Since then the trend has been to discard the piano, to add other instruments (tin whistle, uillean bagpipes, tenor banjo and mandolin) and to do away with rhythm playing by melodic instruments. Instead, all instruments play melody, but at different times and in different combinations to vary the feeling of the tune. Rhythm is provided by the bodhran (pronounced bah-ron), a tambourine shaped drum held vertically and beaten with a two headed stick.

Many of the tunes still played today date from the first flowing of fiddle music in the mid-1700s and have spread to all the English-speaking countries, going through changes in melody and title to suit the times and the region that adopted them. Fiddle music is now subject to a revival among young people in this country, but there are many areas, such as Ireland, Northumberland and the American South, where the music has been played in unbroken tradition since it was first written.

---

1) Before this time the only "rhythm" instrument in the Southern string band was fiddle sticks, which were beaten on a fiddle's strings by a colleague as the fiddler bowed.

A NOTE ON ORNAMENTATION

Players of fiddle music like to embellish or ornament the melody by adding a couple of extra quick notes at certain points in the tune. The points where notes may be added, and the type of embellishment permitted are strictly determined by the regional style the musician is part of or is trying to emulate. New England fiddlers, for example, will occasionally replace a quarter note or two eighths with a triplet ( ) while French Canadian fiddlers tend to do this much more frequently. Irish musicians will use the triplet on hornpipes, but prefer for other types of tunes grace notes ( ) and double grace notes ( ) when the tune is in motion, and rolls when the tune is standing still (holding on the same note for a beat or more).[1] In the arrangements that follow, I have made sparing use of triplets, grace and double grace notes where I felt them absolutely essential. The maxim is always: "When in doubt, don't ornament!"

---

1) A roll involves replacing a quarter note ( ) with two eighth notes of the same pitch ( ), or replacing a dotted quarter ( ) with three eighth notes of the same pitch ( ). As far as fretted instruments are concerned, that's as much as you need to know. (Drowsy Maggie, p. 40, contains some rolls of this type.) In the case of wind instruments or fiddles, two grace notes, one higher and one lower, are interspersed between the eighth notes of the roll, in such a way that the tune seems to be floating in air. Although impossible to notate exactly, a proper roll would look something like this: or . Rolls take their origin from the old bagpipers who, being unable to stop the tone of their instruments, were required to play a quick note of another pitch in between, in order to obtain two notes in a row on the same pitch.

Sean Terrel, Irish tenor banjo player. Photo: Wren d'Antonio

Learning the Necessary Skills

I. *Putting Simple Melodies on a Swing Bass*

The swing bass is an alternating bass with a heavily accented offbeat. Ordinarily, this means that the low E or A strings are struck on the first and third beats of the measure, and that the D string is struck heavily, but only after an ever-so-slight hesitation (hence the swing) on the second and fourth beats. Try it:

Melody notes can be played either on the beat, giving a stationary feel (called a pinch, because that's what you're doing), or between beats, giving a syncopated feel:

(What you have just played is a standard Travis-pattern.)

By judicious placement of pinches and in-betweens, the player makes the piece move interestingly and gives it swing. Another possibility within this style comes from placing a pair of eighth notes on the beat. One of the pair is a melody note and the other is usually another string in the standard chord being fretted. Here's a couple of bars from John Hurt's "Hot Time in the Old Town Tonight" (Vanguard, VSD-79220) using this technique.

I've arranged "Old Joe Clarke," a common tune in the American fiddle repertoire in "Hurt"-style, with only one hammer on thrown in for effect:

Lorraine Lee (dulcimer), author Ken Perlman, & Sara Grey
(banjo) at Indian Neck Festival, Canaan, Connecticut.
Photographer unknown.

Old Joe Clarke

*Key of G Mixolydian
(capo 2 with fiddler)
common time*

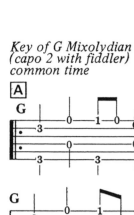

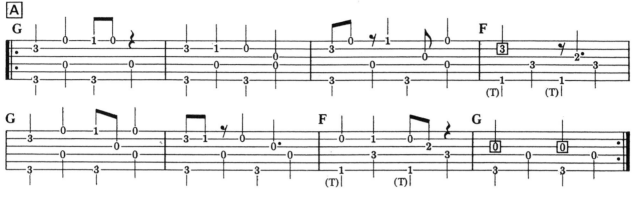

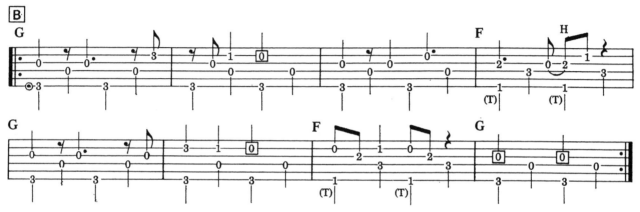

Old Joe Clarke

17

Angeline the Baker

"Angeline" comes from the Galax area of Virginia (in the southwestern part of the state near the North Carolina border). It was first recorded in the late 1920s by Uncle Eck Dunford and can now be heard on a recent Franklin George recording (Kanawa Record Co. No. 307). Play with considerable bounce and spirit. As you play part A, you can sing to yourself:

> "Angeline the Baker, her age is 43
> I buy her candy by the peck but she won't marry me"

Key of D major (tune 6th to D)
common time

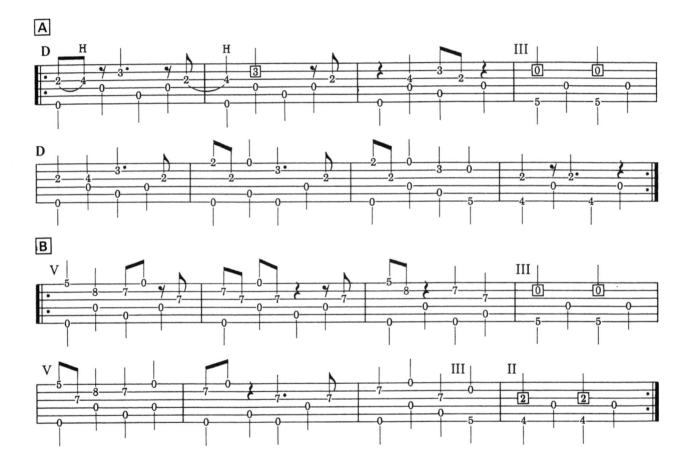

Angeline the Baker

Taylor Kimble, fiddler. Photo: Ray Alden

In most blues and pattern picking, melody is obtained with the right or plucking hand. Hs, Ps and SLs are mostly for ornament. But to obtain the light and rapid feel of dance music, you're going to have to be able to get a lot of the melody (particularly, but not always when two eighth notes follow in succession on the same string) by fretting-hand plucking. Below is a tune "Boatman" that gets some melody through the fretting hand. The swing bass is maintained throughout.

Boatman

Key of G major (6th tuned to D - capo 2 with fiddler)
common time

"Boatman" was collected from Ross Miller of Greenhill, W. Va. by Alan Jabour in the early 1960s, but it was common in American songbooks as early as the 1850s. It is a spirited tune, and can be heard on "Art Rosenbaum and Al Murphy" (Meadowlands No. MS2). Also on "Sarah Grey, with Ed Trickett" (Folk Legacy FSI-38):

Part B: Boatman dance, Boatman sing
Boatman do most anything.

Part C: Dance, Boatman, dance (3 x)
How can I dance with a hole in my pants?

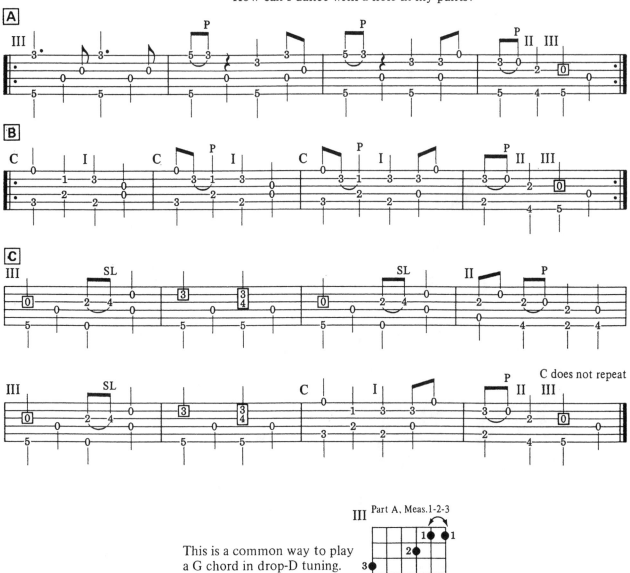

This is a common way to play a G chord in drop-D tuning.

III Part A, Meas. 1-2-3

20

Boatman

Appalachian-style fiddler Alan Jabbour with
author Ken Perlman on banjo. Photo: Susanne Even

In "Georgia Railroad," a considerable part of the melody is obtained by left-hand plucking. It may seem awkward at first, but make sure you get this piece down before you go any further. Note, in part A, the frequent use of partial chords (see diagrams below). This allows for greater mobility and a more interesting sound. Otherwise, the tune is arranged very close to the Hurt style, and the piece "moves" through judicious use of pinches and between-beat notes.

Georgia Railroad

Key of G major
common time

"Georgia Railroad" was first recorded by Gid Tanner and the Skillet Lickers in the 1920s. Both the group and the tune came from northern Georgia, near Atlanta. I've changed the B part a bit to suit the guitar. It can be heard on "Alan Block and Ralph Lee Smith" (Meadowlands No. 1). Spirited and wistful.

Part A: Peter and I went a fishin'
(Georgia railroad, I am bound)
Caught a big mudcat and put it in the kitchen
(Georgia railroad, Georgia gal).

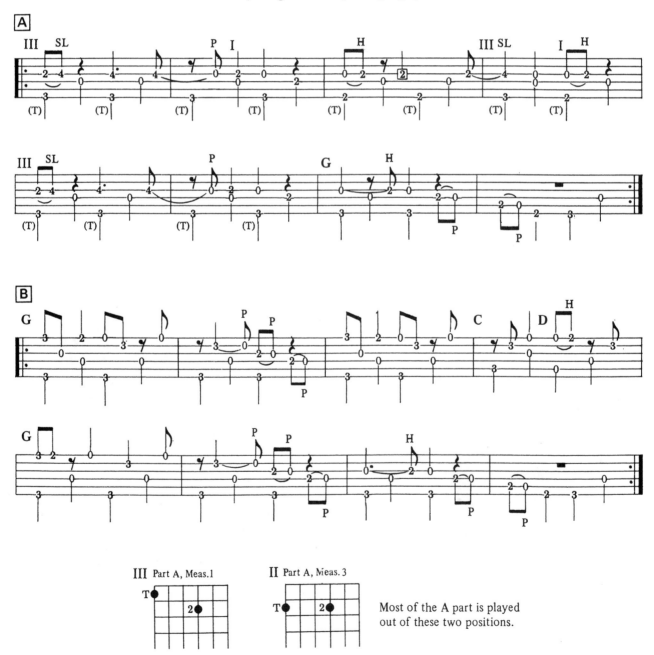

Most of the A part is played
out of these two positions.

Georgia Railroad

III. *Use of Chord Positions to Obtain Melody*

This is a technique Keith-style bluegrass banjo players use constantly. You can fret two or three strings in such a way that you get a run of melody notes by playing them in sequence. In "Cluck Old Hen," you have the figure:

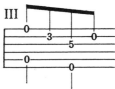

which can be played off the following chord position:

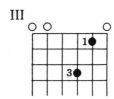

Watch the partial chords throughout (diagrammed below).

Another technique introduced below is getting several notes from a series of Hs and Ps off one struck note. In measure 5 of part A, you strike the first string, fret 3. Then you P to fret 2, H back on to fret 3, and P again to 2. Meanwhile you've kept your bass going and the piece has really taken off! I use this technique whenever I can to make the arrangements float a bit.

Cluck Old Hen

Key of A - Dorian
common time

A song from the deep South, "Cluck Old Hen" was first recorded by the Bog Trotters of Galax, Va. in the 1920s. A reissue of "Al Hopkins and the Hill Billies'" recording of this tune is now on County Records (No. 405). At a moderate pace with a bit of moodiness.

Part A: My old hen's a good old hen,
        She lays eggs for the railroad men.
        Sometimes one, sometimes ten,
        That's enough for the railroad men.

Part B: Cluck old hen, cluck and sing
        You ain't laid an egg since late last spring.
        First time you cackle, you cackle in the lot
        Next time you cackle, you cackle in the pot.

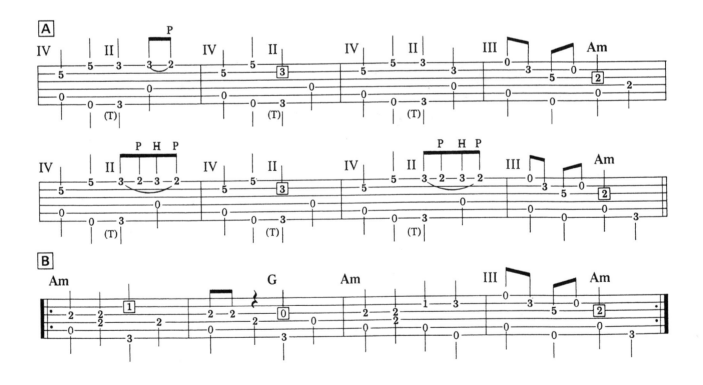

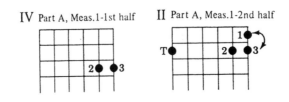

IV Part A, Meas.1-1st half   II Part A, Meas.1-2nd half

24

Cluck Old Hen

Old-time fiddlers at Washington festival. Photo: Suzanne Szasz

IV. *Beyond the Alternating Bass: Playing in Cut Time*

"Jimmy Allen" is an English set tune. It has a strong feeling of two with accent on the first and third beats, so bass notes are only required at those beats. I have diagramed out the partial chords.

Key of G major
Cut time

Jimmy Allen

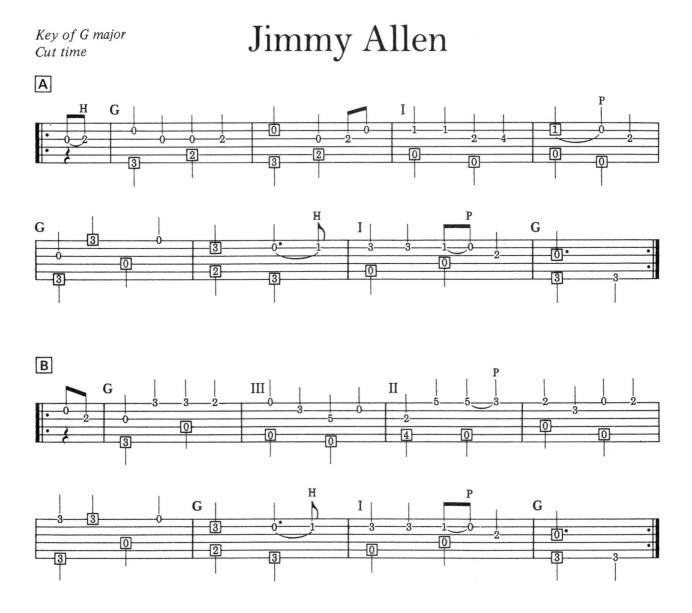

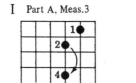 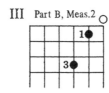 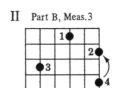

26

Jimmy Allen

V. Phrasing

The jigs, reels and hornpipes are almost unplayable in finger style without a knowledge of phrasing, or note groupings. Most of this must come from listening to musicians who know what they're doing, but I'm going to try to at least give you some understanding of what's involved.

Say we have a reel (such as "Drowsy Maggie, p. 40), and there are eight eighth notes in a measure:

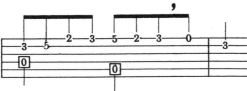

It so happens that here the seventh note is the actual end of the phrase and there is a slight pause at that point. The last note of the measure is actually tied to the first note of the next measure. So instead of:

(DA-da-da-da, DA-da-da-da) - (DOT . . .

The actual sound is:

(DA-da-da-da, DA-da-da) (da-DOT . . .

It makes quite a difference. Be sure to observe all the phrasing symbols.
(NOTE: *The time to shift position is at the phrase mark—not the measure line.*)

VI. Some Additional Things to Know About:

1) *Ornaments*—below are a couple of measures from "The Spanish Lady" (p. 36) in which some grace notes have been placed. As you know (p. 7) grace notes take up no time of their own, but rather absorb some time from the note they're connected to. They are started on the beat (often as a pinch with a thumb note), and some quick left hand plucking gets you back to the

quarter or eighth note they're attached to before it's time to play the next note. The single grace note should be played with a slight explosive quality in Irish music, and takes the form of a very rapid pull off. The double grace note has a "whining" quality, and is a quick H and P (d'd'DOT) coming to rest on a quarter note.

2) *Using the fingers to pluck melody notes on the bass strings*—sometimes the first finger of the right hand must move over to obtain melody notes on the D string. (See the first measure of "Little Beggarman.") In this case the whole hand shifts, the second finger plays the G string and the third plays the B string. Get used to this because it happens a lot in the following pages. Occasionally, there will even be melody notes on the A string that you'll have to get with your first finger. (Then the second finger plays the D string, etc.)

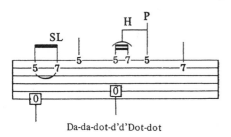

Da-da-dot-d'd'Dot-dot

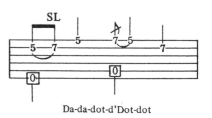

Da-da-dot-d'Dot-dot

The Little Beggar Man

This piece gives you a chance to put some of these new techniques to work. Originally a hornpipe by the name of "The Red-Haired Boy" (see *O'Neill's Music of Ireland*), "The Little Beggarman" has become best known by the title of the wistful lyrics put to it by an anonymous Irishman. Played as a reel in New England, and as a hoedown in the South, it is the probable ancestor of the tunes "Salt River" and "Salt Creek."

Part A: I am a little beggarman a beggin' I have been
I been three score and more on this little Isle of Green
Been down from the Liffey right down to the Sligo (pronounced sleegoo)
And the name that I'm known by is "Old Johnny Dew."

Part B: Of all the trades a goin' out the beggin' is the best
For when a man is tired he can lay him down and rest.
Sit around the fire with nothin' else to do
But dance for your supper with your old rigadoo.

Key of G Mixolydian
common time

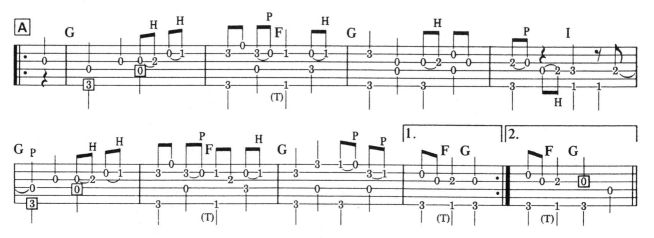

28

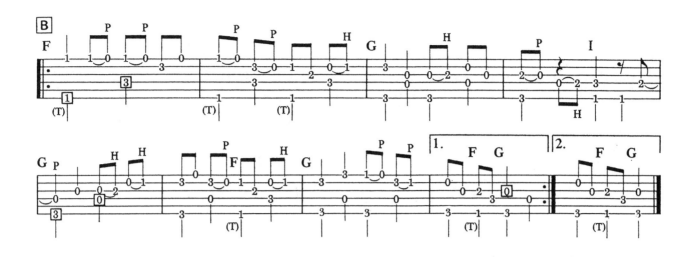

The Little Beggar Man

Hoedowns

Hoedowns have very strong accents on the off beat, (second and fourth) and excepting "Over the Waterfall" (which is in cut time) they've been arranged with a swing bass. To get real old-timey flavor, you should accent the off beat with your fingers as well as with the thumb.

Over the Waterfall

This tune was collected from Henry Reed, a W. Va. fiddler. Reed remembered dancing to it at a circus when he was a child, so the tune in its present form probably dates from the turn of the century. It became so popular with urban old-time musicians that Matty Umanov, the proprietor of a well-known fretted-instrument shop in Greenwich Village. hung a sign prohibiting its being played on the premises. (Also verboten were protest songs, "The Deep River Blues," and "The Maple Leaf Rag.") I think it's a lovely tune. "Over the Waterfall" can be heard on "Art Rosenbaum and Al Murphy" (Meadowlands No. MS2). Spirited with a heavy offbeat.

Key of D major (6th tuned to D)
cut time

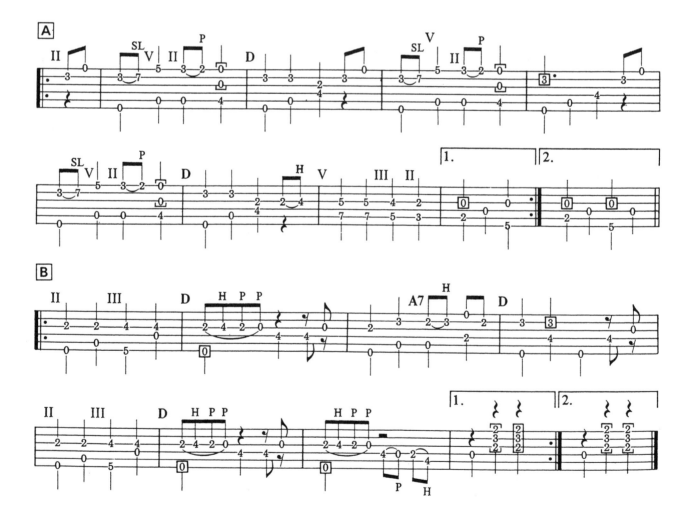

Over the Waterfall

Arkansas Traveller

"Arkansas Traveller" was part of a minstrel routine in the 1850's and probably dates from that period. The "Hey farmer!" routine the New Lost City Ramblers popularized (see *The New Lost City Ramblers' Songbook*), dates from the late nineteenth century:

Q. Hey farmer! Your roof's leakin', why don't you fix it?
A. Well, I can't fix it when it's rainin', and when it don't rain, it don't leak!

Key of C major
(capo 2 with fiddle)
common time

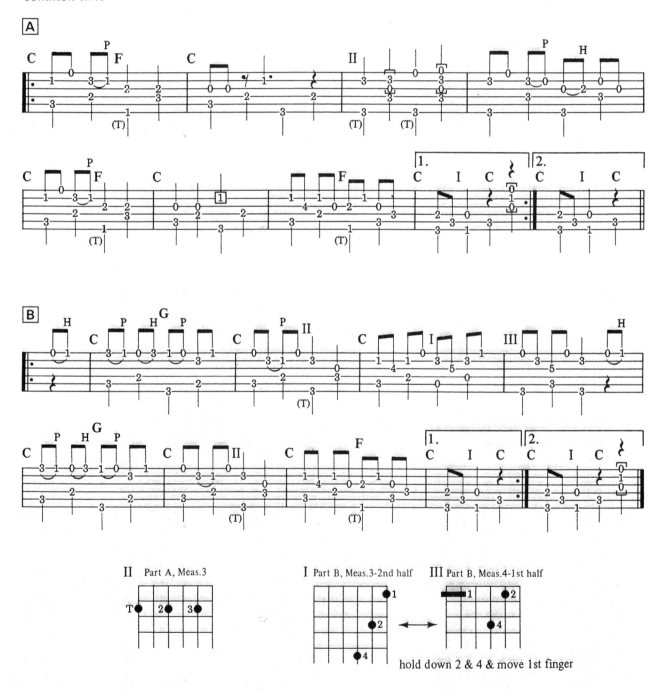

II Part A, Meas.3   I Part B, Meas.3-2nd half   III Part B, Meas.4-1st half

hold down 2 & 4 & move 1st finger

Arkansas Traveller

*Fiddler Houston Galyean with his cousin playing banjo, c. late 1800s,
Near Round Peak, NC. Collection of Ray Alden*

June Apple

Another tune from the Galax area of Virginia, "June Apple" is extremely popular with revival string bands and clawhammer banjo players. Wade Ward does a lovely banjo version on "The Clawhammer Banjo" (County No. 701). Spirited and fast.

Part B: Train on the Island, Hear the whistle blow
Run and tell my true love, I'm sick and I can't go.

Key of G Mixolydian
(capo 2 with fiddler)
common time

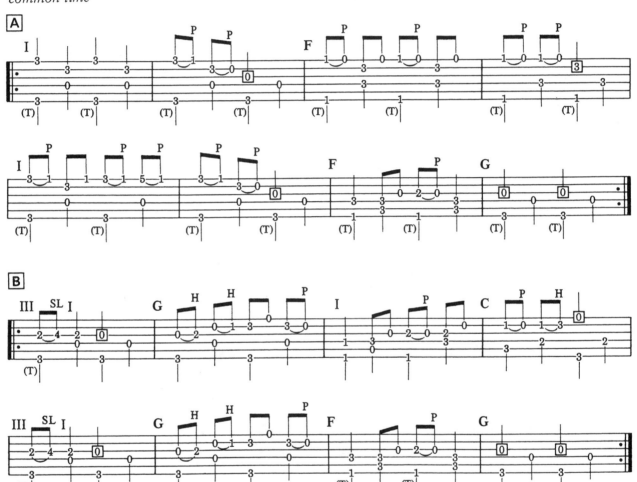

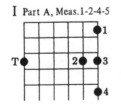

I Part A, Meas.1-2-4-5

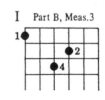

I Part B, Meas.3

June Apple

Dennis Pitre, fiddle, Vincent Doucet, guitar and pianist Irene Gallant from the Tignish area of Prince Edward Island, Canada. Photo: Ken Perlman

Sugar in the Gourd

"Sugar in the Gourd" is known throughout the South and is related to "Turkey in the Straw." The title may derive from the practice of throwing sugar on puncheon (split log) floors to make them smoother for dancing. On "Alan Block and Ralph Lee Smith" (Meadowlands No. MS1). With a lilt and some wistfulness:

Part B: Met her on the road and danced by the board
Tune that they played was the Sugar in the Gourd.
Sugar in the gourd, can't get it out,
Way to get the sugar out—roll the gourd about.

Key of G major
common time

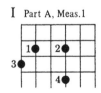

I   Part A, Meas.1

Sugar in the Gourd

*Author Ken Perlman, on stage with Canadian guitarist Ken Brown
at the Fox Valley Folk Festival near Chicago. Photo: Susanne Even*

Whiskey Before Breakfast

"Whiskey Before Breakfast" has been one of my favorite tunes ever since Nick Krukovsky, an Ithaca fiddler and hammer dulcimer player, taught it to me about two years ago. It is closely related to a tune called "Dubuque," and somewhat related to "The Green Fields of America" and "Possum up a Gum Stump." There is some confusion as to its origin, but I've been told that it hails from the Scots part of the Canadian Maritime provinces, where it bears the title "The Spirits of the Morning." It fits the shuffle bow so well that it has become a favorite among Southern-influenced old-timey bands. A foot stomper.

Key of D major
(6th tuned to D)
common time

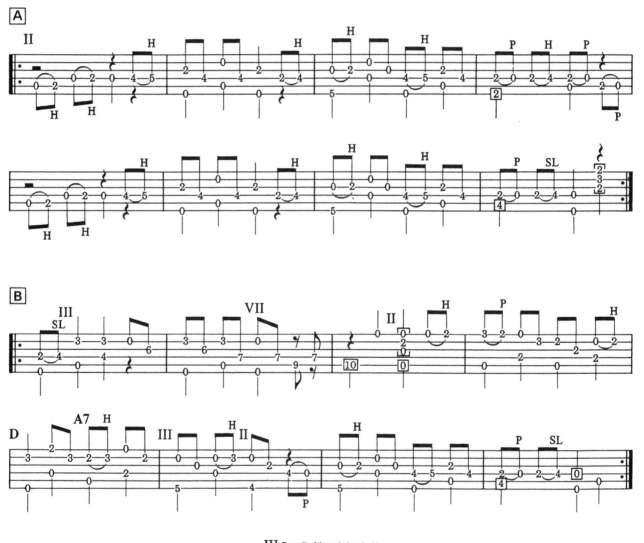

III Part B, Meas. 1-1st half

Whiskey Before Breakfast

Fiddler Attwood O'Connor and guitarist
Stanley Bruce, from the Montague area of Prince
Edward Island, Canada. Photo: Ken Perlman

Reels & Set Tunes

The two set tunes here should be among the first tunes you try. They are, above all, bouncy, and full of good humor.

True reels must be played fairly fast to sound alive. The bass takes on a droning quality, and long strings of Hs, Ps and SLs allow both for the necessary speed and the "liquid" or sliding feel that should occur between notes. Reels usually have eight eighth notes per measure, and quite often the phrase begins at the last eighth note of the preceeding measure. (Reread carefully the section on phrasing, p. 23).

Though a reel is written as:

da Da-da-da-da, Da-da-da-da Da

It often sounds like:

(da-DA-da-da-da, Da-da-da) (da-Da

Irish fiddler Tommy Gallagher, NY. Photo: Wren d'Antonio

The Spanish Lady

This polka (set tune) is now the melody to a popular Irish song. It is descended from a tune called "Doran's Ass," which in turn was drawn from a pipe march named "Mogillemhar" (My Fast Servant). With a lot of bounce, but not a lot of speed. Part B does not repeat.

Key of D major (tune 6th to D)
cut time

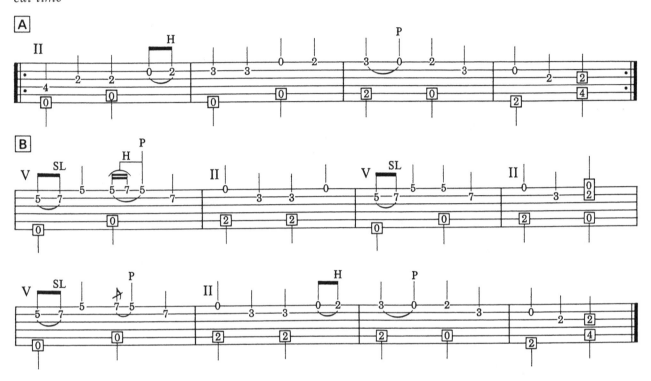

The Spanish Lady

The Rose Tree

This set tune dates from the mid-eighteenth century and is known wherever English is spoken. It is now particularly popular in New England, Ireland (where it is called "Portlairge," for a town on the Republic's East coast) and Scotland (where it is entitled "False Knight on the Road"). In the late 1700s, "The Rose Tree" was featured as a song in *The Poor Soldier Boy*, a play by William Shield (1748-1829):

> Part A: O, the rose tree in full bearing has sweet flowers for to see,
> One rose beyond comparing for beauty attracted me.

> Part B: Though eager once to win it Lovely blooming fresh and gay,
> I find the canker in it and now I throw it far away.

"The Rose Tree" is one of the prettiest tunes I know, and can be heard on "Alan Block and Ralph Lee Smith" (Meadowlands No. MS1). Spirited, at a medium tempo.

Key of D major (6th tuned to D)
cut time

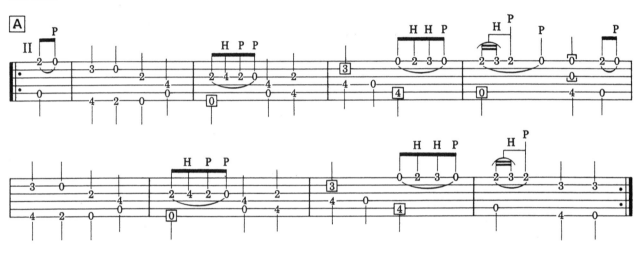

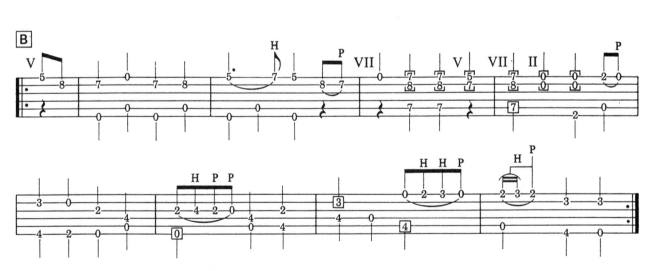

V Part B, Meas. 1

The Rose Tree

Step-dancers at Acadian fiddle festival, Abram-Village,
Prince Edward Island, Canada. Photo: Ken Perlman

Swallowtail Reel

"Swallowtail" dates from the eighteenth century and is still popular in Britain, Ireland and New England. There's a related tune in the key of A mixolydian called "Pigeon on the Gate." In both *O'Neill's Music of Ireland,* and in *The Nelson Collection,* it can be heard on "The Legacy of Michael Coleman" (Shanachie No. 33002). Fast, with "gliss" and attention to phrasing.

Key of A Dorian
cut time

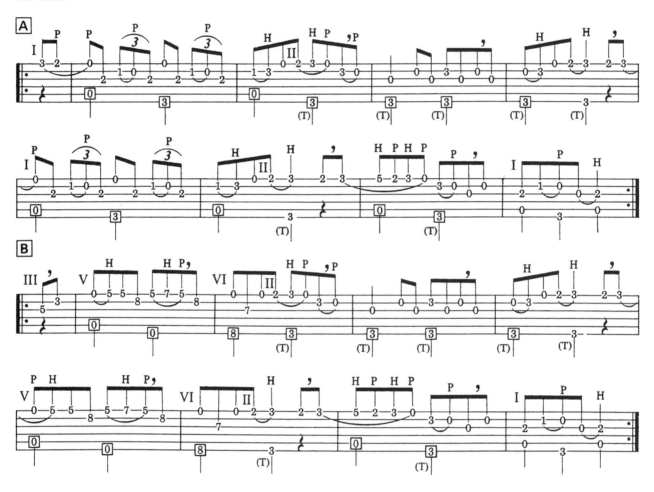

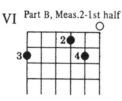

VI   Part B, Meas.2-1st half

Swallowtail Reel

L-R: Jackie Webster, Carl Webster & Donny MacDonald of Cardigan,
Prince Edward Island, Canada. Photo courtesy Earthwatch.

Drowsy Maggie

"Drowsy Maggie" is one of the best known Irish reels. Printed in *O'Neill's Music of Ireland*, it can be heard on "The Chieftains No. 4 (Claddaugh Records No. 8TA10). Very fast, with considerable gliss between notes and much attention to phrasing. Note that each part is played only once.

Keys of E Dorian (Part A)
and D major (Part B)
cut time

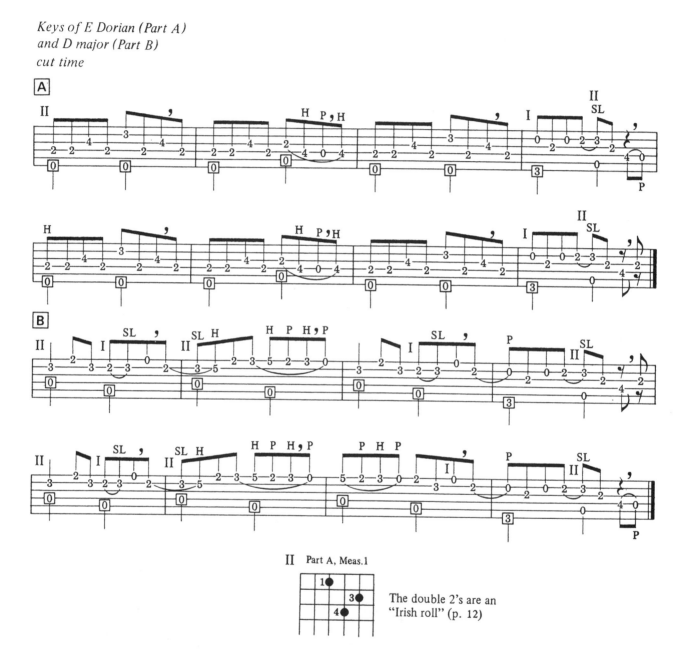

II   Part A, Meas.1

The double 2's are an "Irish roll" (p. 12)

Drowsy Maggie

Eddy Arsenault of St. Chrysostom, Prince Edward Island, Canada. Photo: Ken Perlman

Marches

Marches are stately tunes that cover a wide range of moods. They always have a strong accent on the first beat of each measure and should be played, more or less, at a brisk walk or loping pace.

Young Dublin pipers. Photo: Wren d'Antonio

The Return from Fingal

The word "fingal" comes from the Gaelic term for "territory of the foreigners," here referring to an area near Dublin recaptured from the Danes during the eleventh century. Legend attributes the tune to Brian Boru's harper who is said to have composed it to mourn his master's death at the battle of Clontarf. In *O'Neill's Music of Ireland,* and on "The Chieftains No. 4" (Claddagh Records No. 8TA-10) as part of a set called "the Battle of Aughrim." As you play it keep in your mind's eye a slowly advancing army in medieval dress moving through a misty sunrise.

Key of E Dorian
cut time

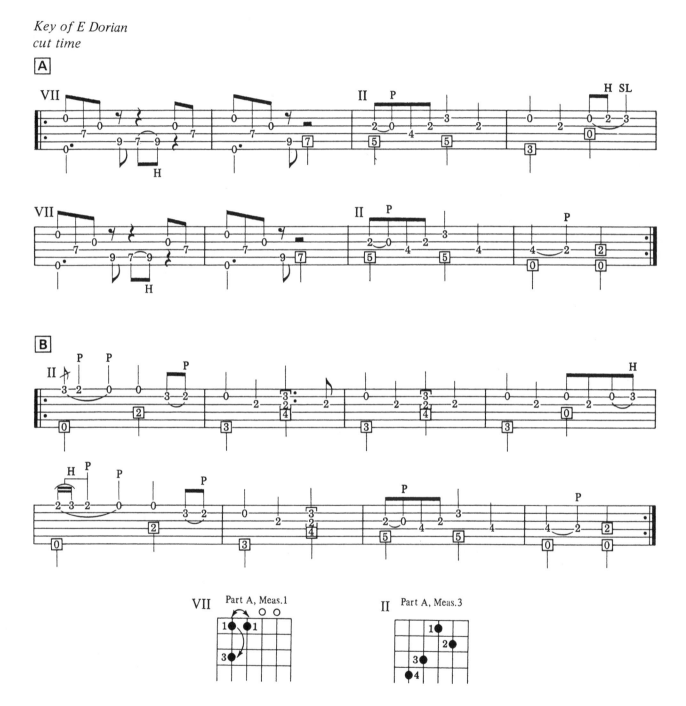

The Return from Fingal

Nancy

50

Nancy

Howie Bursen, a fine clawhammer banjo player, brought this lovely march down to Ithaca one winter's day after a trip to Toronto, and taught it to all of us. It was apparently written by Tom Clough, a Northumbrian piper of the early twentieth century, and is included in one of the Northumberland Pipers tune books. On "Northumbria Forever" (The High Level Ranters-Trailer No. 2007).

Key of D major (6th tuned to D)
cut time

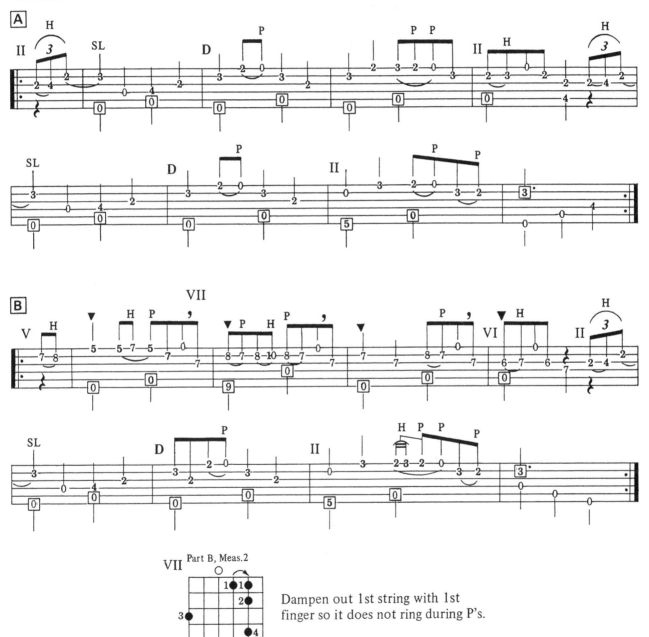

Dampen out 1st string with 1st finger so it does not ring during P's.

The Halting March

This old Irish pipe march is also called "The Wexford Pikemen" and is said to have been used for drilling during the 1798 rebellion against England. On "The Boys of the Lough-Second Album" (Rounder No. 3006). At a loping pace. The accents below are very pointed (staccato-like). Note "B" does *not* repeat.

Key of A Dorian
cut time

52

The Halting March

The Battle of Aughrim

Aughrim (pronounced "okrim"), a town in the Galway region of Ireland, was the site of the last great battle between the English and the Irish in the seventeenth century. Until the development of the uillean (bellows) bagpipes, with its greater range and flexibility, this tune was played exclusively on the flute and fife, having too many notes for the warpipes. On "The Chieftains No. 4" (Claddagh Records No. 8TA-10). A stirring tune. Play at a loping pace with a heavy accent on the first beat of each measure.

Key of A Dorian
cut time

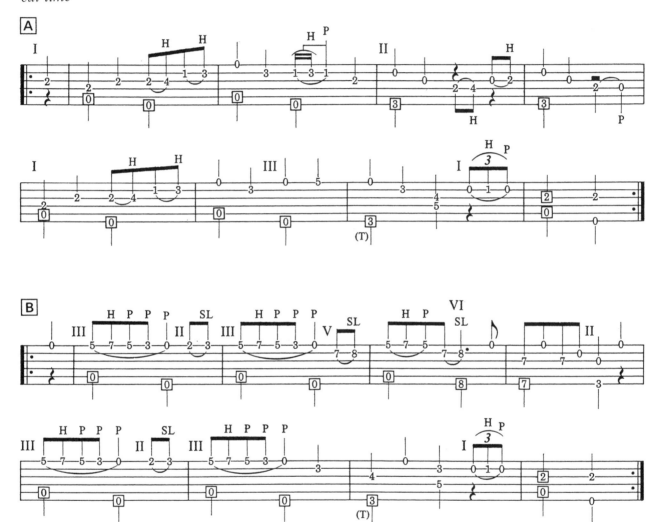

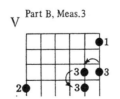

Part B, Meas. 3

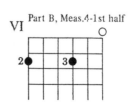

Part B, Meas. 4-1st half

The Battle of Aughrim

Canadian duo Mary Anderson & Ken Brown at the Celtic Roots Festival in Goderich, Ontario. Photo: Ken Perlman

Napoleon Crossing the Rhine

This tune appeared as a "band march" (as opposed to one designed to be played on the pipes of fife), in the early part of the nineteenth century under the above title. Around the Civil War period it became known (outside the South, of course) as "Sherman's March to the Sea." It is now played in the West, where it is called "Napoleon Crossing the Rockies." (There's the folk process for you!) It is written in a true four, which means that there's a whole lot going on in each beat. (That's why there's a lot of sixteenth notes—some troublesome measures are "sounded out" below.) I learned "Napoleon" from Judy Hyman, a fiddler now living in Jeffersonville, N. Y. At a lope, with a lot of spirit and joyfulness. On "Summer Oaks & Porch: The Fuzzy Mountain String Band" (Rounder No. 0035).

Key of D major
(6th tuned to D)
common time (4/4)

Napoleon Crossing the Rhine

The Kings County Fiddlers' Association, led by Fr. Charles Cheverie, performs at the Rollo Bay Fiddle Festival in Prince Edward Island, Canada. Photo: Ken Perlman"

Some fiddlers and accompanists from eastern Prince Edward Island. L-R: Margaret Ross MacKinnon, Clare McDonald, Leonard McDonald, Ward MacDonald, Allan MacDonald, Attwood O'Connor & Peter Chaisson. Photo: Ken Perlman

Hornpipes

When I was just getting into fiddle music, most of the tunes I chose to learn later turned out to be hornpipes. They are the "prettiest" of the fiddle tunes and, to paraphrase Scott Joplin, "Do not play these tunes fast. It is never right to play hornpipes fast!"

Hornpipes are played with a more or less "dotted" feel (DOT-da, DOT-da obtainable by hitting the first note of the dotted pair a bit harder than the second), and have two major accent points per measure (on the first and third beats) around which two distinct phrases (see p. 23) are often built.

So, although hornpipes are written as:

da   DOT-da-dot-da,   DOT-da-dot-da,   Dot

They often are played like:

(da-DOT-da-dot)   (da-DOT-da-dot)   (da-Dot

Remember to shift position at the change of phrase, and to be conscious of special accent points, which take on great importance in hornpipes.

Northumbrian fiddler. Courtesy of the British Information Service.

The Boys of Blue Hill

A favorite among Irish musicians and popular in New England as well, this tune dates from the early nineteenth century. It is known in most of England and Scotland as "The Beaux of Oak Hill" and in Northumberland as "The Boys of North Tyne," while in Virginia, a slightly simplified version is played as a hoedown and called "Keep the Ark a-Movin'." ("The Fuzzy Mountain String Band"-Rounder No. 0010). Gordon Bok plays a finger-style version of "The Boys of Blue Hill" on "A Tune for November" (Folk-Legacy No. FSI-40) as part of a medley he calls "Lou's Handy." At a moderate speed, with very close attention to phrasing.

(tune 6th to D)
cut time

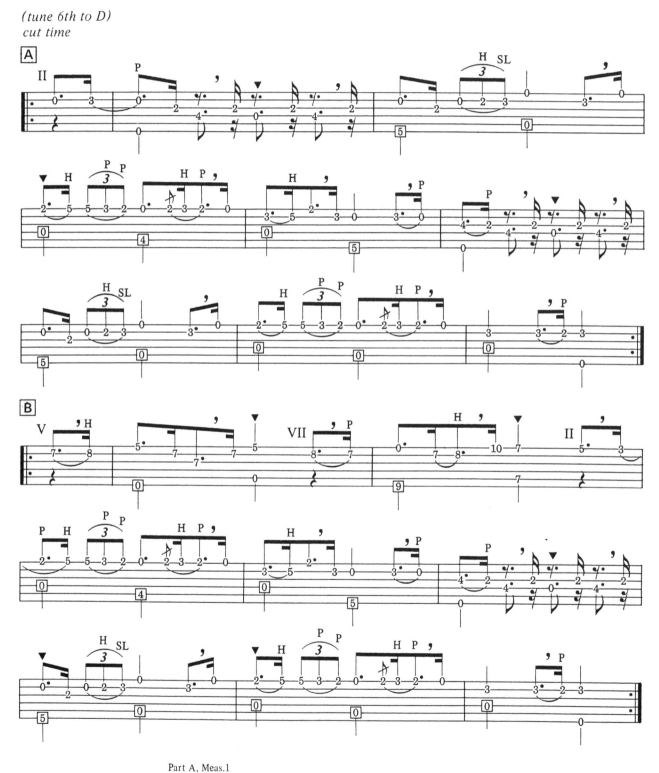

Part A, Meas.1

= a dotted pair with the thumb playing the dotted eighth and the finger playing the sixteenth.

The Boys of Blue Hill

The Rights of Man

Popular in Britain, Ireland and New England, "The Rights of Man" was probably written as a tribute to Thomas Paine's famous pamphlet of the 1790s. A beautiful and haunting tune when played slow and with attention to phrasing. Printed in *Allen's Irish Fiddler,* it can be heard on "The Hammer Dulcimer: Bill Spence and the Fennigs All-Star Band" (Fronthall Records No. 01).

Key of E Aeolian
cut time

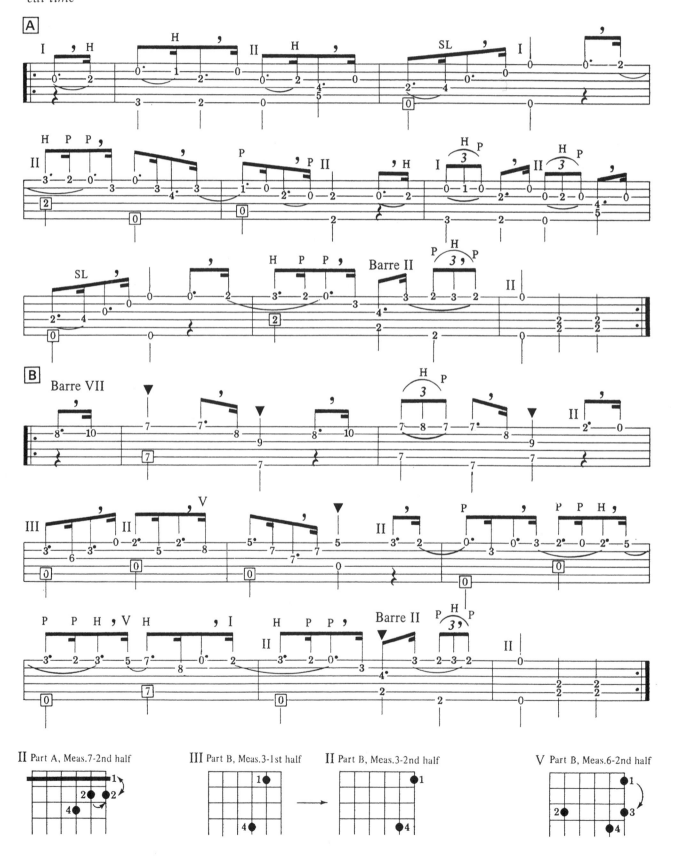

The Rights of Man

Fisher's Hornpipe

This tune was probably written by an English composer named John Christian Fischer (1733-1800). It is still played as a hornpipe in Britain and Ireland, but New Englanders play it as a reel, and Southern fiddlers play it as a hoedown with a strong offbeat. (See the March/April 1975 edition of Sing Out! Magazine, Vol. 24, No. 1, for my finger picking arrangement of "Fisher's" more in the Southern style.) Printed in *O'Neill's Music of Ireland*, and in Cole's *1000 Fiddle Tunes*. "Fisher's" should be played spiritedly, but not heavily dotted.

Key of D major
(6th tuned to D)
cut time

Fisher's Hornpipe

The Flowers of Edinburgh

This piece has been popular in New England (where it is now played as a reel), Britain, and Ireland since the middle of the eighteenth century. "Flowers" was a euphemism of that period for "sewers," so this tune was written as a good natured joke about a city its composer (very likely a Scotsman) had a lot of affection for. In *O'Neill's Music of Ireland,* in Cole's *1000 Fiddle Tunes,* and on "Jean Carignan" (Folkways No. FG3531). Medium speed but spirited, with very close attention to phrasing. Not heavily dotted. Remember to shift at the phrasemarks, not at the measure lines!

Key of G major
cut time

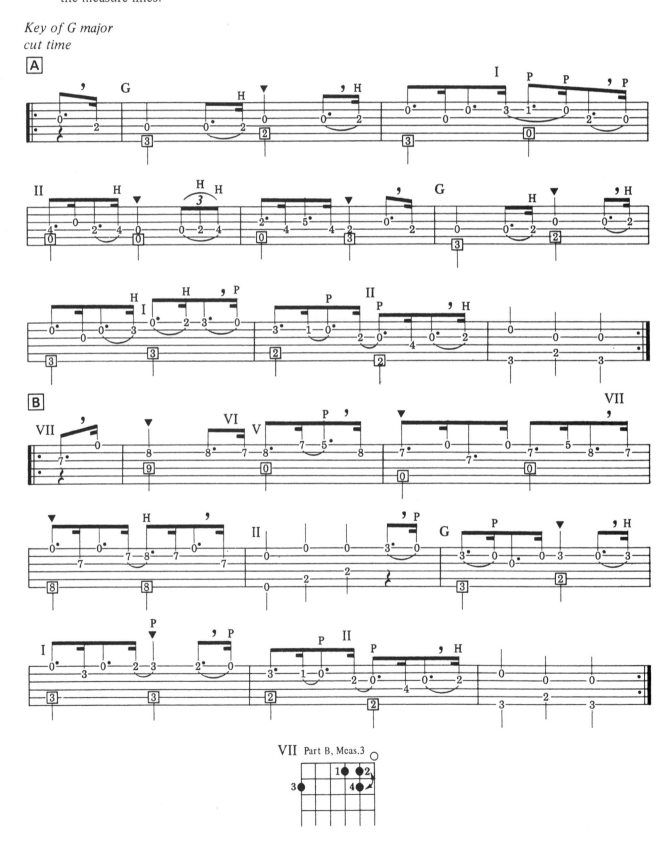

VII   Part B, Meas.3

The Flowers of Edinburgh

Marcus Welsh, bodhran, and Packy Russell, concertina.
Photo: © Ann Blackstock

Jigs (& Slides)

Jigs are written in 6/8 time, which means they can have as many as six eighth notes per measure. These are arranged as two groups of three with the accent on the first of each group:

Da-da-da, Da-da-da

A quarter note can be substituted for any two eighth notes, yielding something very similar to a dotted pair:

(DOT-da, DOT-da)

A note to be held for the duration of one of the above groups (or) will be written as a "dotted quarter."

Most jig melodies are made up of combinations of eighth note groups ( ) and quarter-eighth combinations ( ), but those made up mostly of ( ) are called single jigs, while those composed primarily of ( ) are known as double jigs.

Knowledge of phrasing, while particularly important for the slides (see note, p. 63) is also necessary for the playing of true jigs. Usually, a note grouping written as:

(Da-da-da, Da-da-da) (DOT

will be played: (Da-da-da, Da-da) (da-DOT-

Watch those accent points (▼)! They really make jigs come alive.

68

The Road to Lisdoonvarna

I learned this haunting single jig, bearing the name of a town in County Clare (in the West of Ireland), from Greg Ryan, a mandolinist and tin whistler now sojourning in New York. There is a reel of the same name with which it is often played as a "set." In the *Armagh Pipers Tune Book*, and on "The Chieftains No. 3 (Claddagh records No. TA5). At a slow lope with heavy accents where marked.

Key of E Dorian
6/8 time

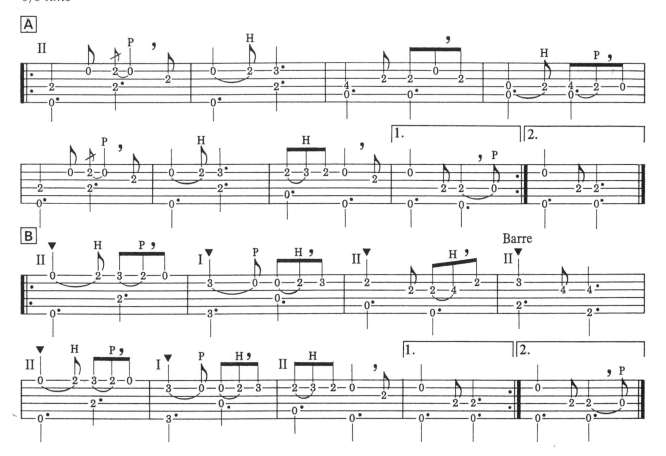

The Road to Lisdoonvarna

Whistle player in Dublin. Photo: © Andrew Courtney

Famed Canadian fiddler Don Messer c. 1950 with his band the Islanders. Photo courtesy Prince Edward Island Public Archives and Records Office.

O'Keefe's Slide

A slide is a type of single jig in which the major accent occurs every other measure, making it properly in 12/8 time, instead of 6/8.[1] It comes from Kerry, an area in the southern tip of Ireland. O'Keefe was a famous Kerry fiddler of this century (died c. 1950), and this tune, its original title forgotten, became known by his name. In the *Armagh Pipers Tune Book* and on "The Chieftains No. 4" (Claddagh No. 8TA-10). A haunting melody when played at a loping pace with attention to accents and phrasing.

Key of A Dorian
6/8 time

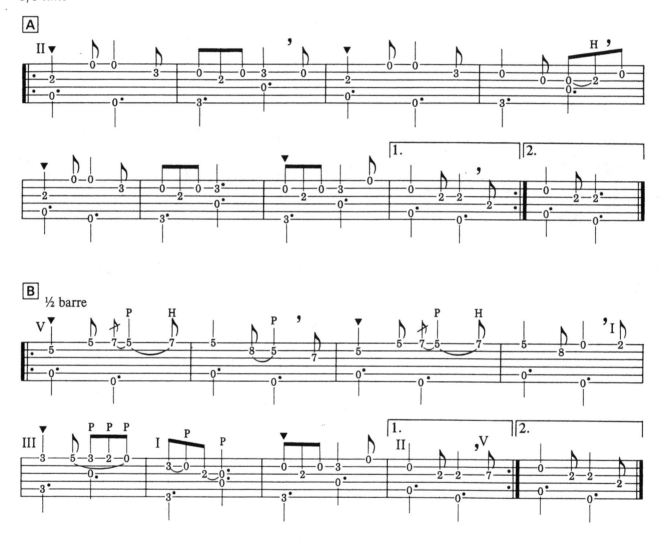

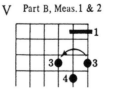

V   Part B, Meas.1 & 2

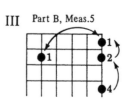

III   Part B, Meas.5

---

1) Slides are written in 6/8 even though they are played in 12/8.

O'Keefe's Slide

Fiddler Stephen Toole of Bonshaw, Prince Edward Island.
Photo: Ken Perlman

Elsie Marley

Elsie was the wife of an eighteenth century Northumbrian innkeeper. Her wit and good spirits attracted the trade of men from all ranks of society. A local musician and wag wrote the following tune and some humorous but sympathetic lyrics when a small accident befell her, probably due to excessive drinking of the juice of the barley. "Elsie Marley" was first printed in *Ritzen's Bishopric Garland* in 1784, and is now in *The Northumberland Pipers Tune Book*. I learned it from Eric Mintz, an Ithaca, N. Y. clawhammer banjo and concertina player.

Part A: Do ya ken Elsie Marley, henney,
    The wife that sells the barley, honey.
    She lost her pocket and all of her money
    Behind in the bush in the garden.

Part B: Elsie Marley, she's so fine,
    She won't get up to feed the swine,
    She lies in bed till eight or nine,
    Oh surely she does take her time.

Key of G Mixolydian
6/8 time

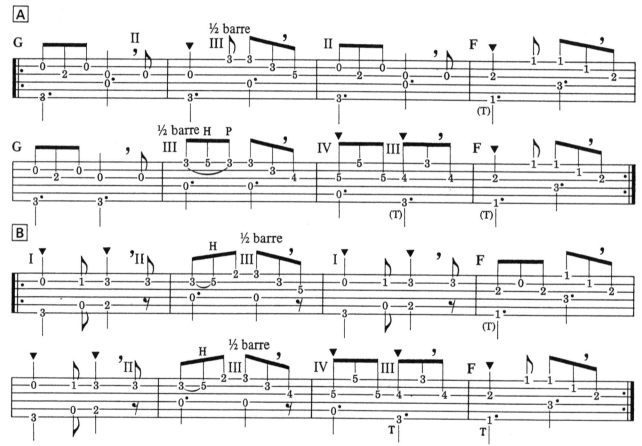

III Part A, Meas.2-2nd half

Elsie Marley

Costumed concertina player at Northumbrian festival. Photo: Brian Shuel

Haste to the Wedding

A double jig, "Haste" was first published in the mid-eighteenth century with the title "Rural Felicity." Played all over Britain and Ireland, it is very popular in New England, and is even known by some Southern fiddlers. In Cole's *1000 Fiddle Tunes*, O'Neill's *Music of Ireland* and on "Jean Carignan" (Folkways No. FG3531). At a medium tempo, with a bounce. Those accents are important!

Key of D major
(6th tuned to D)
6/8 time

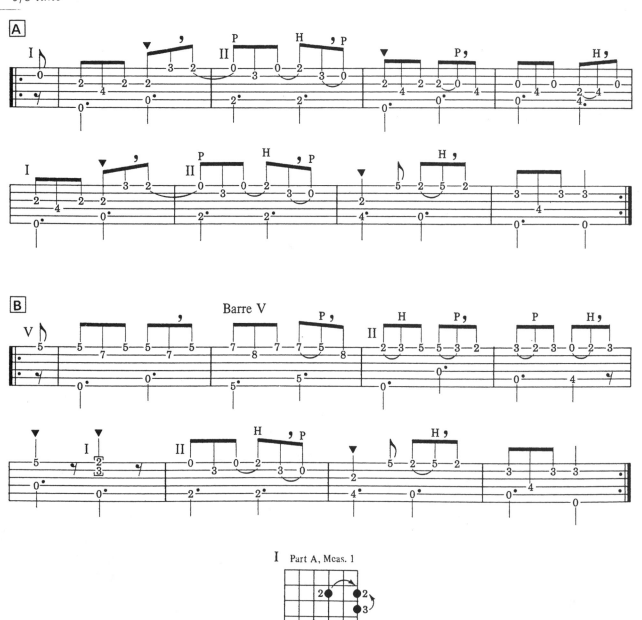

I   Part A, Meas. 1

Haste to the Wedding

Canadian fiddling champion Pierre Shryer (center) with band members at the Celtic Roots Festival in Goderich Ontario. Photo: Ken Perlman

Some 3/4 Times Tunes

If you can count to 3, you shouldn't have any trouble with this section. A measure can have as many as three quarter notes, the accent always being on the *first* note:

(DOT-dot-dot), (DOT-dot-dot)

A half-note takes up the space of two quarters:

(Dot - - - dot) or (DOT-dot - - -)

and a dotted half fills an entire measure:

Two eighth notes can be substituted for any quarter note, and may be strung together to a maximum number of six:

(Da-da-dot-dot) or ((Dot-da-da-da-da) or (Da-da-da-da-da-da .

The best way to deal with a 3/4 piece is to tap your foot only on the first beat of each measure (repeating "two, three" very softly to yourself after each tap): ONE (two-three) ONE (two-three).

So, if a tune (like part A of "Sonny's Mazurka") has eight measures (x 3 = 24 beats), your foot should tap only eight times, and *a listener will hear only eight beats.* (Think again of a swinging pendulum. Each swing contains an entire 3/4 measure.)

Site of Celtic worship, Ireland. Photo: Wren d'Antonio

Sheebeg Agus Sheemore

This aire is said to be the first composition of O'Carolan, a famous Irish harper of the early eighteenth century. It depicts the aftermath of a battle between two bands of fairies (one living in the big hill—the other in the little), that occurred, according to legend, due to an argument over which hill contained the remains of Finn MacKool, a famous Irish hero. Slow, but not funereal, with a relatively strong beat at the beginning of each measure.

Key of D Major
(6th tuned to D)
3/4 time

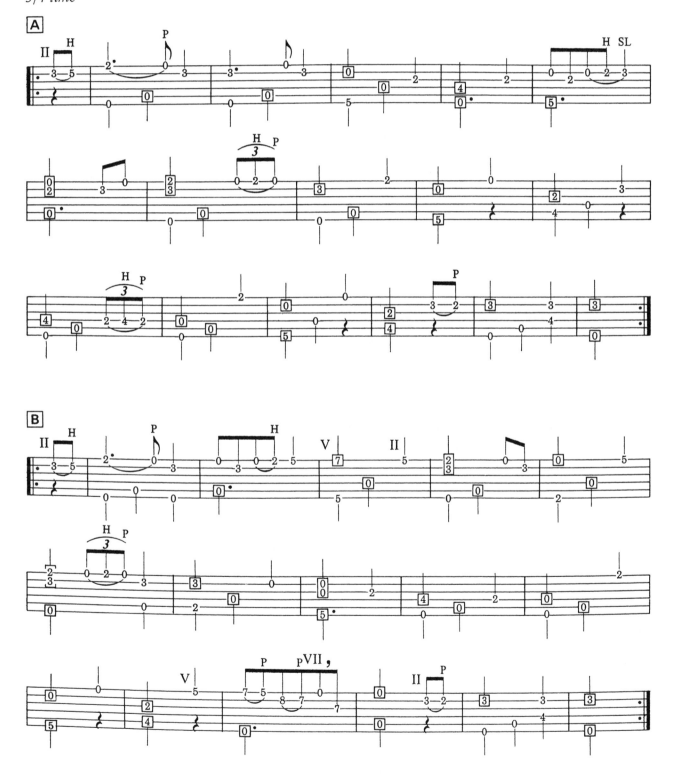

Sheebeg Agus Sheemore

Sonny's Mazurka

Named for Sonny Brogan, a well-known button accordion player of this century, this tune has *very* strong accents on the first beat of each measure and should be played spiritedly. On "The Chieftains No. 3" (Claddagh Records No. TA5). Medium tempo with attention to phrasing.

Key of D major (tune 6th to D)
3/4 time

Sonny's Mazurka

Supplement to the Centerstream Edition

Now that you've mastered many of the skills and concepts involved in fingerpicking fiddle tunes on guitar, try your hand at playing some of the tunes I've recorded over the years. Each of my LPs and CDs – Clawhammer *Banjo and Fingerstyle Guitar Solos, Devil in the Kitchen, Island Boy* and *Northern Banjo* – is represented below by at least a couple of numbers. In addition to the tunes that appear below, five other transcriptions of tunes I have recorded have been published in books. These are *Taylor's Twist, Swingin' on a Gate* and *O'Carolan's Welcome* (all in *Advanced Fingerstyle Guitar*), *Planxty Lord Inchiquin* (in *Fingerstyle Guitar*) and *The Return to Fingal* (in this volume).

As noted in the Preface, I've adopted a few more streamlined notational practices for these more recent transcriptions. To begin with, in the standard notation versions I no longer include position markers (Roman numerals above the staff), or "H" and "P" indications. In terms of the latter practice, the presumption is that the presence of a slur sign plus an assessment of the notes involved should be sufficient to indicate whether an H or P is called for. Another change for both tab and standard versions is that – following standard notational conventions for guitar music – ornaments in the treble are lined up to the *left* of the "full-fledged" bass note to which they are related, rather than being placed directly above it (regardless of how they are written, ornaments should be played as a "pinch" with the corresponding bass note).

Strathspeys

Three of the new tunes are examples of a genre you have not yet encountered in this book: the *strathspey* (pronounced struth-SPAY). Strathspeys are distinctly Scottish dance tunes in 4/4 time. There are two common formats: some have two eight-measure sections; while others have one repeated four-measure section followed by a non-repeated eight measure section.

Of the dance tune categories you are already familiar with, strathspeys most resemble hornpipes. Like hornpipes, strathspeys are played at fairly slow tempos and there are usually eight eighth notes per measure. One major difference is that while hornpipes are played in 2/2 or cut time (notes organized as two groups of four), strathspeys are in true 4/4 time with eighth notes organized as *four groups of two*. A good speed for strathspeys is a metronome setting of about ($\downarrow$) = 132. Only *one fourth* of each measure is played per click.

Also like hornpipes, most strathspey eighth notes are written in the form of *dotted pairs*. A dotted pair is written as a dotted eighth-note plus a sixteenth-note, implying that the first note is three times as long as the second (Example 1a). In Scotland, dotted pairs in strathspeys are usually played pretty much as they are written. In Cape Breton, Prince Edward Island and other parts of Atlantic Canada where the tunes are also played in folk tradition, the notes are played so that the first note of a dotted pair is only *twice* as long as the second, becoming in effect a triplet with the first two notes tied (Example 1b), or – more elegantly – a quarter plus eighth under a triplet bracket (Examples 1c).

Example 1

(a)   (b)   (c)

Example 2

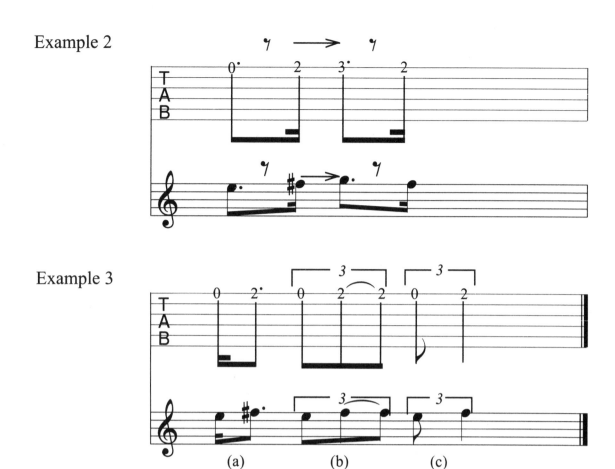

Example 3

(a)   (b)   (c)

In terms of phrasing, each dotted pair in a strathspey is usually played so that the second note (that is, the note written as a sixteenth note) *leads on* to the first note of the *next* dotted pair (or whatever other kind of note occupies the *following* beat, see Example 2). If you play your dotted pairs with the sixteenth note connected to the *preceding* dotted eighth (as is customary in hornpipe playing), the tune loses its character.

Strathspeys often contain several different kinds of notes besides dotted pairs – most notably quarter notes, eighth-note triplets, sixteenth-note groups and a kind of note pair known as the *Scotch snap*. Scotch snaps are essentially reverse dotted pairs. In other words, they are written as a sixteenth-note plus a dotted eighth-note (Example 3a). Again, in Scotland the pair is played more or less as written, but in North American traditions the second note of the Scotch Snap is only twice as long as the first note. This yields a triplet with the last two notes tied (Example 3b), which can also be written as a eighth-quarter combination under a triplet bracket (Example 3c).

Airs

Sometimes called *slow airs* or *fiddle airs*, these are tunes meant for listening rather than dancing You've already encountered one such tune in this book *(Sheebeg Agus Sheemore)*, and there are three more among the tunes in this new section. Airs can have any time signature, and feature a wide variety of tempos, ranging from extremely slow and mournful to spritely. There is a tendency among players well versed in fiddling traditions to play airs with a certain amount of *rubato* (rhythmic freedom). In other words, the melody is often allowed to "breathe" between phrases, and there is a certain amount of ebb and flow in the tempo.

The Humours of Ballyloughlin

Named for a small Irish village, this four-part jig is one of the most striking explorations of the Mixolydian mode found in the Celtic tradition. I learned it in the late 70s when I was working as accompanist for Irish fiddler Kathleen Collins; this setting – recorded on *Clawhammer Banjo and Fingerstyle Guitar Solos* – is deeply influenced by the way she played the tune.

Key: D Mixolydian
Tuning: 6th String to D

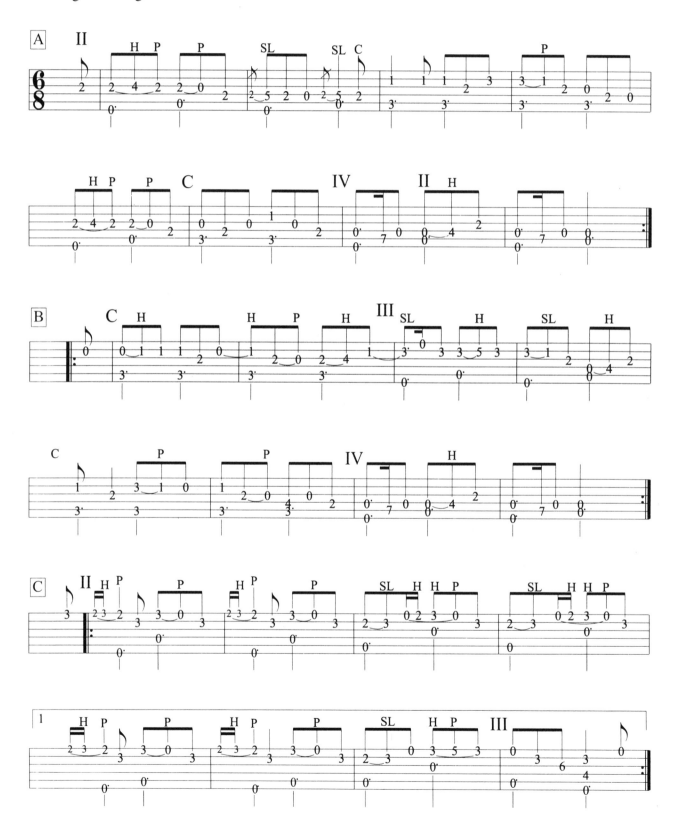

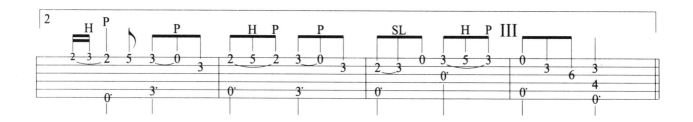

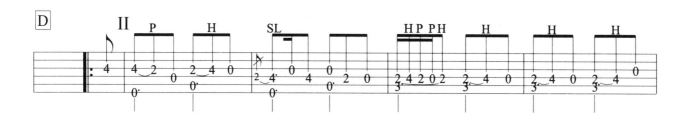

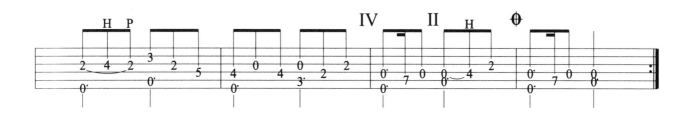

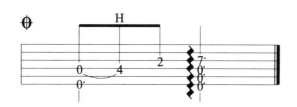

The Humours of Ballyloughlin

Johnny Cronin, Kerry-style Irish fiddler, NY. Photo: Wren d'Antonio

Madame Bonaparte

The Irish have long had a special fondness for the memory of Napoleon Bonaparte, resulting in a whole slew of tunes named for the French conqueror and his associates. This particular tune is roughly in hornpipe style, but with an extended B-part (12-bars instead of the usual 8). These extra bars are indicative that a specific dance with a 40-bar structure (instead of the usual 32-bar form) was dance to this tune. The version presented here – from *Clawhammer Banjo and Fingerstyle Guitar Solos* – is patterned after a recording by the well-known group, the Chieftains.

Key: A Major
Tuning: Standard

Madame Bonaparte

Coilesfield House

This cut from *Devil in the Kitchen* represents a style of medley known as a *Scottish set*: it's made up of three kinds of tunes: air, strathspey and reel. *Coilesfield House* is an air by Nathaniel Gow (1763-1831), scion of a well-known family of Scottish tune-composers and fiddlers. The strathspey is very unusual, and I've never heard anyone play it besides John Campbell, a Cape Breton fiddler who lives in Watertown, Massachusetts (I didn't name the tune on the recording, but I've given it this "working title" for publication). *Loch Earn* is an old Scottish reel, dating to at least the late eighteenth century.

Key: G and G modal
Tuning: Standard

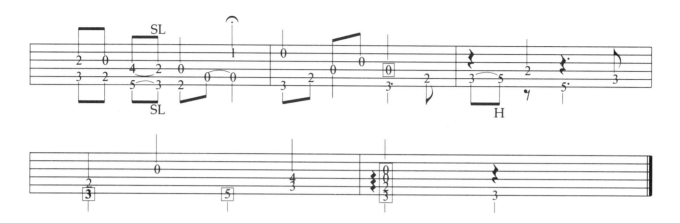

Fiddler Sid Baglole and pianist Margaret Ross MacKinnon
of Prince Edward Island, Canada. Photo: Ken Perlman

Coilesfield House

John Campbell's Strathspey

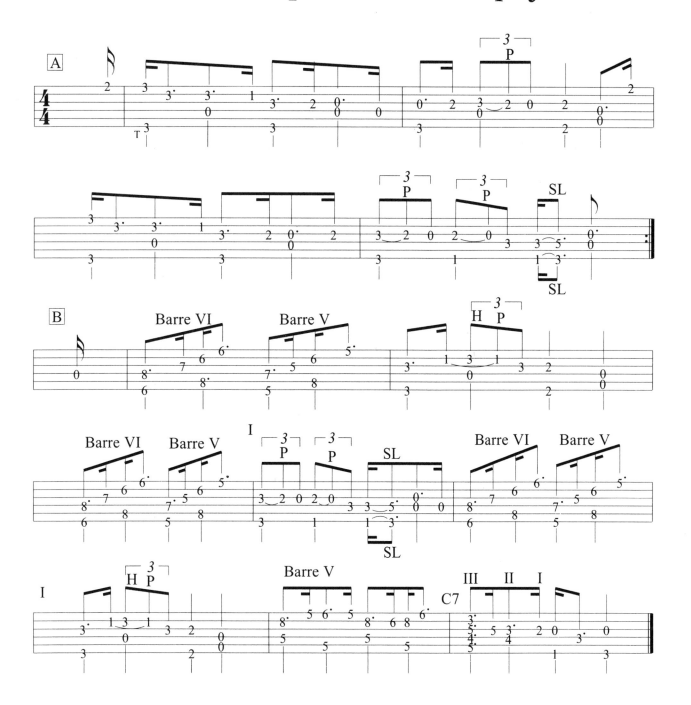

John Campbell's Strathspey

Loch Earn

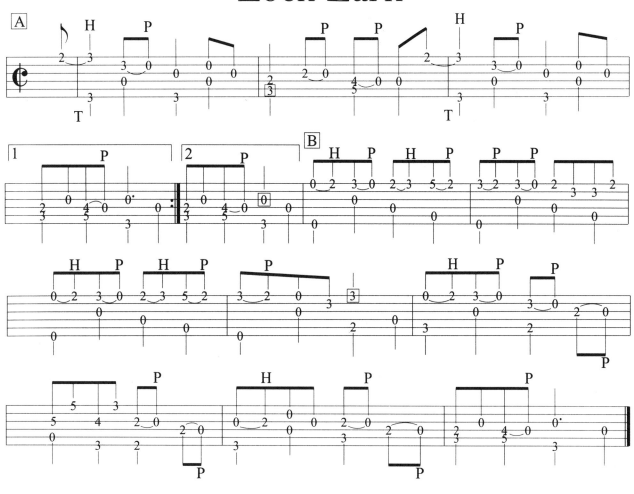

Loch Earn

Professor Blackie

This lovely air and variation (which I recorded on my *Devil in the Kitchen* CD) was written by James Scott Skinner (1843-1927), the last of the great Scottish fiddle music composers. Skinner dedicated it to a Gaelic scholar of his day. I learned the tune from Joe Cormier, the noted Cape Breton fiddler who lives in Waltham, Massachusetts.

Key: D Major
Tuning: 6th String to D

6th to D

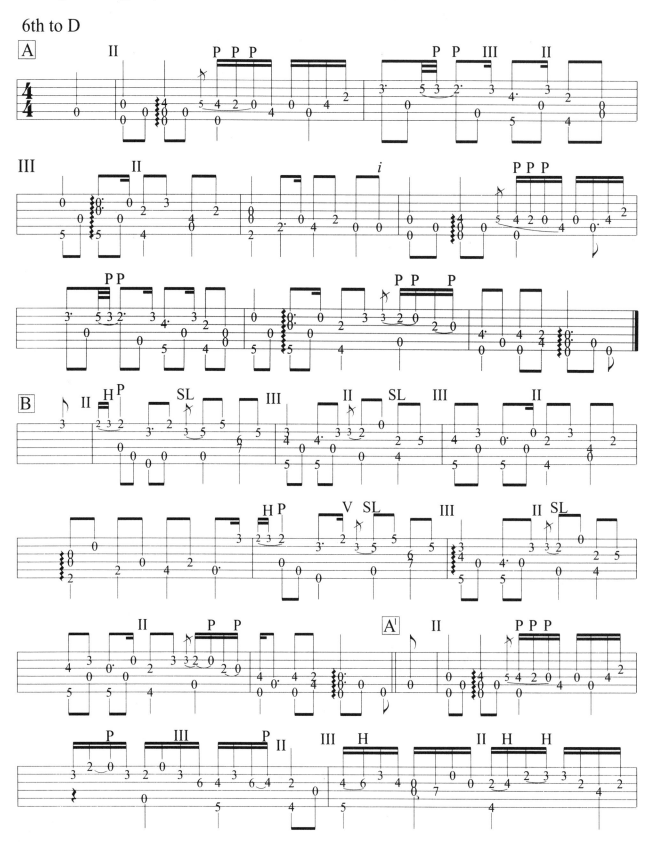

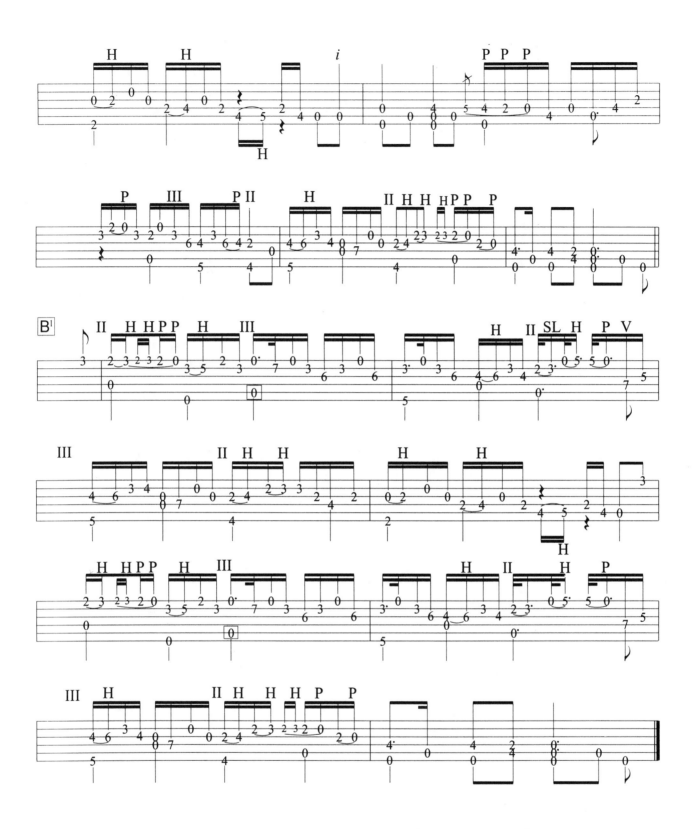

Professor Blackie

Glenfiddich Strathspey

The tradition of playing strathspey and reel together goes back to 18th century Scotland, when this kind of medley was used to accompany a dance known as the *Scotch Reel.* In contemporary Cape Breton, the strathspey-reel medley is typically used to accompany step dancing (clogging). I learned these tunes from "Young Peter" Chaisson, of Bear River, Prince Edward Island (right across the Gulf of St. Lawrence from Cape Breton). When I recorded them on my *Island Boy* CD, I tried to translate to guitar some of the stately grace of his fiddle settings.

Key: D Major
Tuning: 6th String to D

6th to D

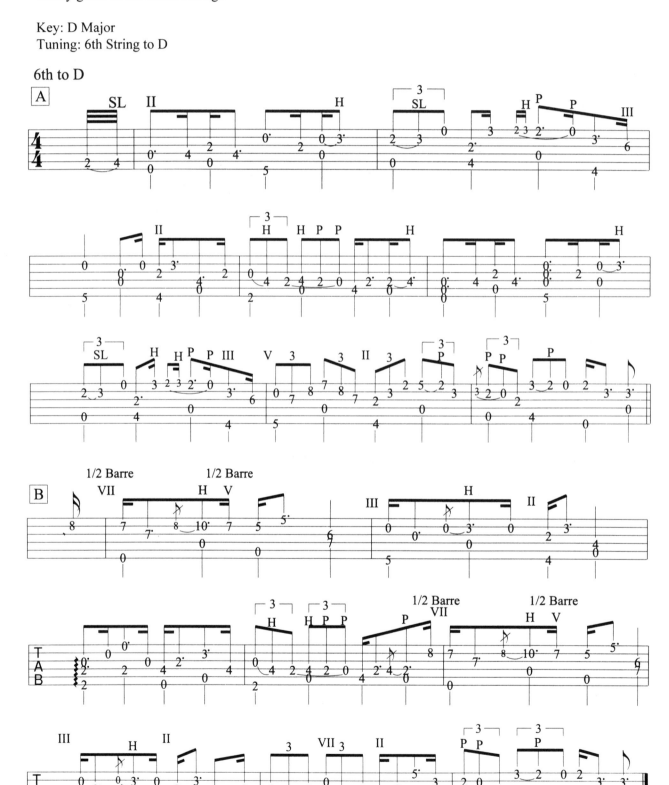

Glenfiddich Strathspey

Homeward Bound

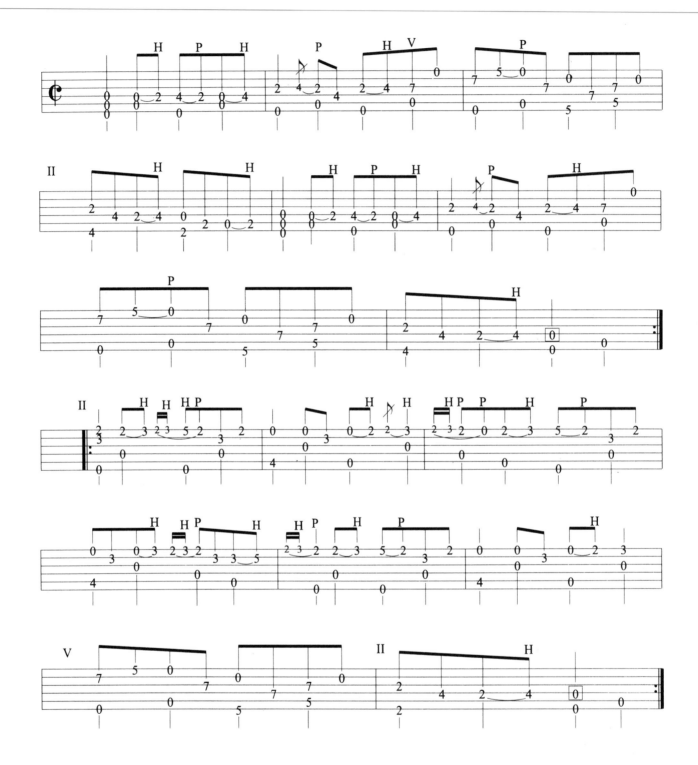

Homeward Bound

The Sweetness of Mary

This medley is from my *Northern Banjo* CD. I dedicate the first tune – written in the last couple of generations by Cape Bretoner Joan MacDonald Boes – to sweet Marys everywhere! The tune is a *slow strathspey*, which means it has the strathspey form but is generally played like an *air* with some degree of *rubato*. Mason's *Apron* – which dates to eighteenth century Scotland – is one of the most widely played fiddle tunes of all time. The variation is dedicated to Irish fiddler Sean McGuire of Belfast, whose many variations on "Mason's" set the modern standard.

Key: A major
Tuning: Standard

The Sweetness of Mary

Mason's Apron

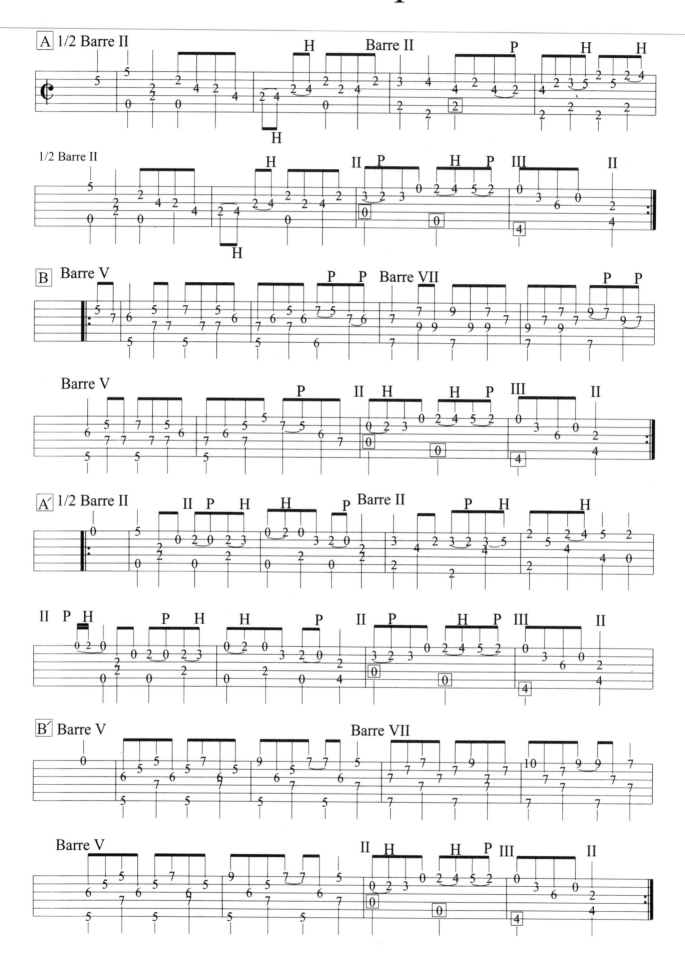

Mason's Apron

Niel Gow's Lament for His Second Wife

This is the best-known composition of well-known 18th century Scottish fiddler and composer Niel Gow (father of the Nathaniel Gow who wrote *Coilesfield House*). In its original printed source, there appears the following inscription: "They lived together thirty years. She died two years before him and left no issue." I learned this tune from Cape Breton fiddler Joe Cormier of Watertown, Massachusetts. My own version – which I recorded on *Northern Banjo* – is also influenced by the interpretations of contemporary Scottish fiddlers, most notably that of Angus Grant of Fort William, Scotland.

Key: D Major
Tuning: 6th String to D

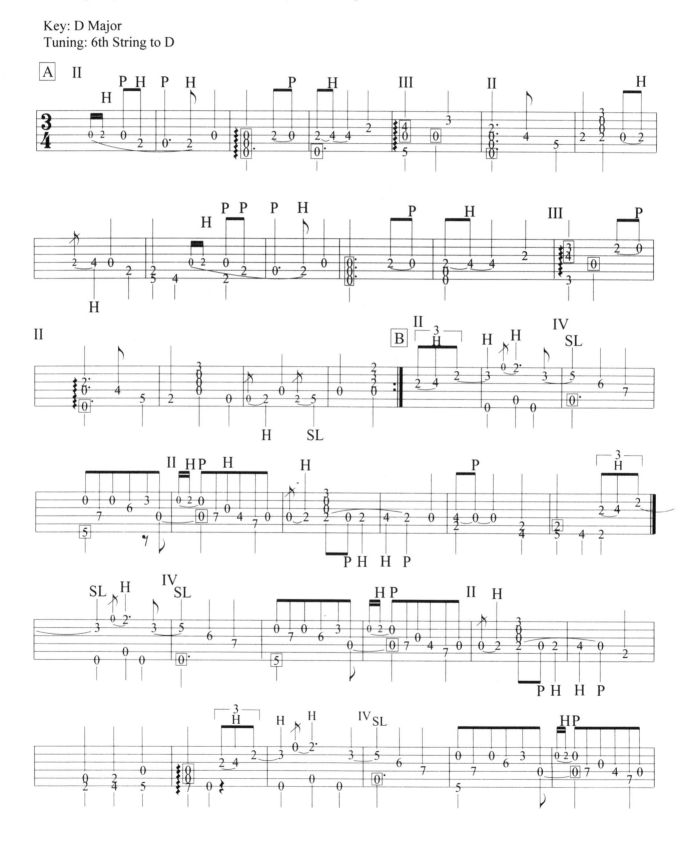

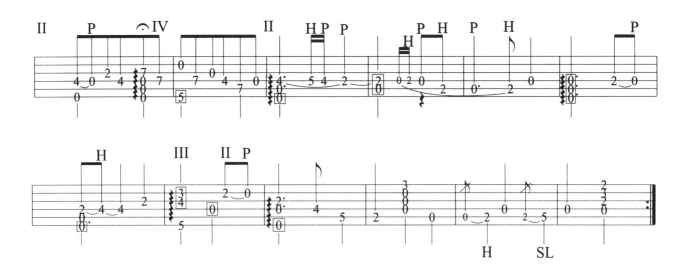

Author Ken Perlman in the late 1970s when the original edition of this book was written. Photo: Wren D'Antonio

Niel Gow's Lament for His Second Wife

6th to D

Scottish Highlands near the Isle of Skye. Many Scholars believe that reels originated in this region. Photo: Ken Perlman

Irish countryside around Cashel. Jigs did not originate in Ireland, but they found their greatest flowering there. Photo: Ken Perlman

Annotated Bibliography

Irish Fiddle Tune Collections:

Allan's Irish Fiddler, Glasgow, Scotland: Mozart Allan Co. Irish standards from the first half of the 20th century.
Learn to Play the Tin Whistle with the Armagh Piper Club. Vols. 1,2&3. Belfast, Ireland: Appletree Press.
   Contains many Irish tunes popular among session-musicians of the 1960's and 70s.
O'Neill, Capt. Francis. *O'Neill's Music of Ireland.* 1903. Collected by the Chicago Chief of Police from local Irish Immigrants.
   With 1,850 tunes, this book is a must for students of Irish music.
Roche Collection of Traditional Irish Music, The. 1912. Cork: Ossian Publications, 1982. Another important turn of the century Irish collection.

North American Fiddle Tune Collections:

Christeson, R.P. *The Old-Time Fiddler's Repertory.* Columbia, Mo: University of Missouri Press, 1973.
   Fiddle tunes collected in Missouri in the 1940's and 50s.
Cohen, John and Mike Seeger. *The New Lost City Ramblers Song Book.* New York: Oak Publications, 1964.
Dunlay, Kate and David Greenberg. *Traditional Celtic Violin Music of Cape Breton.* Toronto: DunGreen Music 1996.
   Transcribed from old 78s recorded by renowned Cape Breton fiddlers.
One Thousand Fiddle Tunes. An excellent source for New England music of the mid-to-late 19th century.
   Recently re-published under its original title, *Ryan's Mammoth Collection* (Mel Bay).
Perlman, Ken *The Fiddle Music of Price Edward Island: Celtic and Acadian Tunes in Living Tradition.*
   Pacific, MO: Mel Bay, Inc., 1996. 425 transcriptions from field recordings of traditional fiddlers

Scottish and English Fiddle Tune Collections:

Kerr's collection of Merry Melodies for the Violin. 4 vols. Glasgow: James S. Kerr. Reprint of an 1870's work.
MacDonald, Keith Norman. *The Skye Collection.* 1887. This and the *Athole Collection* (below) are consideredthe two classic Scottish tune-books.
*Northumberland Pipers Tune Book, The .*Tyne and Wear, England: Northumberland Pipers Society.
Skinner, James Scott. *The Scottish Violinist.* Glasgow, 1900.
Stewart-Robinson, James. *The Athole Collection.* 1884. See note for the *Skye Collection* (above).

General Works:

Breathnach, Breandán. *Folk Music and Dances of Ireland.* Cork: Mercier Press, 1971.
Collinson, Francis. *The Traditional and National Music of Scotland.* Knoxville: Vanderbilt University Press, 1966.
Emmerson, George. *Rantin' Pipe and Tremblin' String.* 1972 2nd ed. London, Ontario:Galt House, 1988
Sharp, Cecil J. *The English Folk Song: Some Conclusions.* London, 1907.
   contains an excellent discussion of modes and other aspects of traditional music.
Wolfe, Charles. *The Devil's Box: Masters of Southern Fiddling.* Nashville: Vanderbilt University Press, 1977.

Discography

Alan Block and Ralph Lee Smith (Meadowlands #MS-1)
The Boys of the Lough: Second Album (Rounder #3006)
John Campbell: Cape Breton Violin Music (Rounder #7003)
Jean Carignan: Old Time Fiddle Tunes Played by (Folkways #FG3531)
The Chieftains Nos. 1,2,3,and 4 (Claddagh #TA3, TA4, TA5, and TA10)
Angus Chisholm: The Early Recordings of (Shanachie #4401)
The Clawhammer Banjo (County #701)
Melodic Clawhammer Banjo (Kicking Mule #209)
Michael Coleman: The Legacy of (Shanachie #33002)
Joseph Cormier: Scottish Violin Music from Cape Breton Island
   (Rounder #7001)
The Fuzzy Mountain String Band (Rounder #0010)
   Summer Oaks & Porch: (Rounder #0035)
Angus Grant: Highland Fiddle (Topic #12TS347)

Sarah Grey with Ed Trickett (Fok Legacy #FSI-38)
Gordon Bok: A Tune for November (Folk Legacy #FSI-40)
The High Level Ranters: Northumbria Forever (Trailer Record #2007)
Al Hopkins and the Hill Billies (County #405)
Ken Perlman: Island Boy (Wizmak),
   Clawhammer Banjo &Fingerstyle Guitar Solos (Folkways #31098)
   Devil in the Kitchen (Marimac),
   Northern Banjo (Copper Creek)
The Price Edward Island Style of Fiddling:
   Fiddlers of Eastern P.E.I. (Rounder #7015)
   Fiddlers of Western P.E.I. (Rounder #7014)
Art Rosenbaum and Al Murphy (Meadowlands #MS2)
Mike Seeger: Old Time Country Music (Folkways #2325)

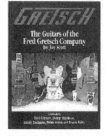